The
Art of
Golf
ANTIQUES

The Art of **Golf ANTIQUES**

An Illustrated History of Clubs, Balls, and Accessories

by Gilbert King
Photographs by Bruce Curtis

In cooperation
with the USGA
Museum

COURAGE BOOKS

An Imprint of Running Press Book Publishers
PHILADELPHIA • LONDON

9 8 7 6 5 4 3 2 1

Digit on the right indicates the number of this printing

Library of Congress Cataloging-in-Publication Number 00-135499

ISBN 0-7624-0990-8

Photographs © 2001 by Bruce Curtis

Cover design by Bill Jones
Interior design by Rosemary Tottoroto
Edited by Molly Jay and Victoria Hyun
Typography: Palatino

This book may be ordered by mail from the publisher.
But try your bookstore first!

Published by Courage Books, an imprint of
Running Press Book Publishers
125 South Twenty-second Street
Philadelphia, Pennsylvania 19103-4399

Visit us on the web!
www.runningpress.com

The author would like to thank the United States Golf Association for its participation and assistance in making this book possible. Particularly, Andy Mutch and Nancy Stulack of the U.S.G.A. Museum in Fair Hills, New Jersey, who were extraordinarily generous with their time and efforts. Rand Jerris at the U.S.G.A. Library was also of invaluable assistance in the research stage of this project. —*Gilbert King*

I would like to acknowledge Andy Mutch and Nancy Stulack of the United States Golf Association; John Foster; Tara Dalrymple; John Wheatley; W.W. Carrath, Sr.; Jay Morelli; Graham Lenny of the St. Andrews Golf Links Trust; and Jay Nieporte of the Winged Foot Golf Club. — *Bruce Curtis*

Anything from antique golf trophies to scorecards from noteworthy tournaments or courses will get the attention of the serious collector.

INTRODUCTION

An assortment of woods and irons from 1900–1906 when hickory
shafts were the standard shaft on most clubs.

The game of golf has traditionally surged in popularity from time to time in its glorious history. Sometimes it was because of a lapsed edict. In 1457, King James II of Scotland banned golf because the country was at war with England, and it appeared that his soldiers were neglecting their archery practice to partake in the ancient Scottish game of golf. When James IV demonstrated a significant addiction to the links courses himself, and the war with England ended, the Scots took to the game with a vengeance and never looked back.

Sometimes golf surged in popularity because of a ball, such as when the inexpensive gutta percha was developed in the mid-nineteenth century. Gutties replaced the expensive feathery balls and enabled the masses to play rather than just the royal and wealthy. The game expanded into the countrysides and clubmaking became an industry.

But sometimes, the surge in golf could be attributed to a man. In 1900, a British golfer by the name of Harry Vardon crossed the Atlantic for a nine month barnstorming tour of America. Vardon was already an Open Champion and legend in Europe, but the soft-spoken Brit caused a sensation ("Vardonmania") in the United States upon his arrival. His every round was front page news, and when his tour brought him to New York City they closed the Stock Exchange in his honor. It was a British invasion of a different sort, and the impact on the younger generation of Americans was deep and lasting.

A year after Vardon returned to Europe, a golf prodigy named Robert Tyre Jones, Jr. also known as Bobby Jones,

Hickory was primarily used in making shafts from 1900–1906.

was born in Georgia. Jones would ultimately achieve unprecedented success on the golf course and his dignity and grace made him the most revered athlete of his era—an era that included Babe Ruth, Jack Dempsey and Red Grange. Upon his death in 1971, the famed sportswriter Grantland Rice wrote, "Whatever any future giant of the links does to par, no one will ever replace Bobby Jones in the hearts of those to whom golf means more than a game."

The integrity and aura of Bobby Jones also had a lasting impact on the sport, an even greater contribution than his extraordinary Grand Slam conquest. Later on, great golfers such as Ben Hogan, Arnold Palmer and Jack Nicklaus would give golf another jolt, bringing the game to new levels of popularity and increasing the lure and mystique of golf.

The full effect remains to be seen, but it goes without saying that the most current surge in the popularity of golf can be attributed to Tiger Woods. Woods burst onto the golf scene as a child prodigy, laughing it up with Bob Hope on television at the age of three, hitting balls inappropriately long and straight for a child of his age. He

Novices can start their collections on a shoestring budget and still find their own piece of golf history.

would go on to win three straight amateur championships before turning professional at the age of 20 in 1996, and just four years later his accomplishments, particularly in golf's major tournaments, have created a "Tigermania" the sport has not seen in perhaps a century.

With public interest in golf at such a fever pitch, it is no surprise that antique golf collectors are thrilled as well, as they see the value of their collections growing by leaps and bounds. Like the gutty ball which brought golf to the masses, the internet has made it possible for anyone to do an eBay search for antique golf collectibles and begin collecting themselves! A recent "eBay" search by the author revealed an Old Tom Morris putter selling for $1,400 and a few Tiger Woods golf cards listed for over $3,000. Novices can start their collections on a shoestring budget and still find their own piece of golf history. From the Schenectady putter to the next yet-to-be-discovered "Troon Clubs," there's a great deal of the game's past out there somewhere. The intent of this book is to give both serious and novice collectors an understanding of some of golf's most treasured collectibles and how they came to be.

Golf trophies are still popular collectibles because they display well on any collector's shelves.

A BRIEF
HISTORY
OF THE
GAME

Ben Hogan wore these shoes, noted for the extra spikes, in 1951
when he won the U.S. Open at Oakland Hills.

Perhaps you've seen the commercial. Tiger Woods blasts his golf ball across the streets, buildings and parks of New York City, and ultimately sinks a putt into a paper cup on the Brooklyn Bridge. It might seem like nothing more than some ad man's contrived attempt to urbanize golf and market the game as exciting and explosive, rather than one which generally takes place in a more pastoral setting.

In fact, Tiger's "street" game in Manhattan is closer to the origins of golf than one might imagine. In the late 13th century, the Dutch were actually playing a game called golf where players would hit hard wooden balls toward targets such as the doors of windmills, courthouses and castles around town. (Casks of beer to the winner, too!) In their passion for long and challenging matches, they would march through cemeteries and centers of town, often having to clear pedestrians from their target sights, much to the dismay of the citizens, who sometimes suffered broken windows and even bones as a result of errant shots! What could be more exciting and explosive than that?

To effectively pinpoint the exact origin of golf as we know it today, it is important to take into consideration history's proliferation of stick and ball games. There may indeed have been hundreds of variations on games that bear some resemblance to golf. There are ancient Greek murals portraying men engaged in games that appear to be closer to what we now consider field hockey as far back as the 5th century B.C. And in fact, the Romans used a ball that was very close to the feathery, a pagani-

An assortment of smooth-faced irons pre-1895.

ca, which was a leather ball stuffed with feathers or hair in a game that appears to be related to handball.

If a ball such as the paganica existed in those ancient times, it seems entirely possible that someone thought to use it in a stick and ball game as well, perhaps even in some early form of golf itself. Yet, without knowledge of the types of clubs or rules of these games, we can only speculate. There are records as far back as the year 872 when King Alfred of England was coronated in which some sort of game was made of "driving balls wide over fields." Clearly, at some point, a man with a stick in his hand and a stationary ball must have had the imagina-

tion to test his strength and accuracy by hitting the ball to some distant target without some type of "defender" present to impede his stroke. And perhaps this early "feathery" ball took flight in a way not unlike a golf ball of today, and the thrill of a solidly struck shot excited this man. Perhaps he hit the sweet spot, immediately took notice, and set about looking for ways to make his shot better. Maybe he discovered that a lofted clubface produced more height on his shot. The speculation is endless. But it does not seem beyond the realm of possibility that some form of golf was probably being played long before history can document its existence.

Clubs used by Walter Hagen in the 1919 U.S. Open.

Ben Hogan's driver, used in U.S. Open competition.

Photographic portraits of golfers are another popular collectible.

REMINISCENCES
OF

GOLF

ON

ST. ANDREWS LINKS

BY

JAMES BALFOUR

EDINBURGH: DAVID DOUGLAS

1887

PRICE ONE SHILLING.

HINTS on PLAY
with
STEEL SHAFTS

by
HENRY COTTON

PRICE 25
SPA[LDING]
"Red Cover" Se[ries]

HOW
TO
PLAY
GOLF

BY
JAMES BRAID
AND
HARRY VARDON

AMERICAN SPORTS PUBLISHING CO.
21 Warren Street, New York.

MY

THE
GAME
OF
GOLF

Since almost every major tour player has written one, golf instruction books
have always been popular collector's items.

The main reason there is any documentation at all of golf is because the game apparently created a great deal of havoc among the Dutch citizenry. There was so much collateral damage caused by golf players (windows of houses and churches were broken, not to mention sometimes significant injuries to pedestrians) that city and country officials were forced to put laws on the books curtailing the more harmful aspects of the game.

The game of golf apparently went like this: four players from each team took turns hitting a wooden ball toward the intended target, with the winner determined by the fewest number of strokes needed. The earliest game on record, a match on Boxing Day in 1297, took place at the Castle of Kronenberg, near the town of Loenen aan de Vecht. The targets were the door of a windmill, a kitchen door, the door of a castle and the door of a courthouse. Incidentally, the game continued to be played annually on Boxing Day for nearly 550 years until 1831, when the Castle of Kronenberg was demolished, and so vanished one of the holes!

At some point, because of the above described collateral damage, the game of golf was moved to open grounds to steer clear of buildings and bystanders. Games were played on a rectangular court with grass apparently kept short by the archers who also made use of the grounds. A tree appears to have been the target the players worked toward, now that castle doors and the like were prohibited. Golf became a more peaceful and pastoral game, rather than the noisy and destructive version villagers had come to know and be bothered by.

Still photos of Byron Nelson's swing at impact in 1949, as well as swing sequence photos of Julius Boros in 1959.

By the 15th century, golf must have exploded if the amount of ordinances noted on public records are any indication. Orders about compensation for damages relating to mishit balls show up in many towns and cities, as do laws prohibiting the game being played near churches and churchyards. If you were caught in Amsterdam in 1480, for example, playing golf near a street named Nes, you'd have to forfeit your clothes right there on the spot!

In the beginning of the 16th century, golfers were likely to be the subject in portraits and sketches by Dutch painters. In the *Book of Hours* located in the British Museum, a golfer is portrayed in the act of putting while he is kneeling amidst three other players. It is also interesting to note that the game was most popular during the seasons other than summer, since that is the time of year that the grass grew to be the longest. In fact, golf was often played on ice, and many drawings and paintings depict the game in this fashion.

At around the same time in the 16th century, portraits of children with a golf club and ball became a popular form of depiction, further indication that the game was quite popular at the time. We also know that the demand for clubs and balls was increasing, as villages such as

In 1588, during the Spanish war, the village of Tilburg was held ransom for 12,000 balls!

Goirle and Delft were commonly described as "ball-stuffers" since their output of golf balls was so significant. In fact, on record in 1588 during the Spanish war, the village of Tilburg was held ransom by an army commander (Sebastian van Warendorp of the Duke of Parma) for 12,000 balls! Tilburg was unable to produce that many balls on such short notice. But their neighbors in Goirle were able to provide a 6,500 ball installment, preventing Tilburg from being burned to the ground!

It is also of note to mention that there is, on record, something of an environmental concern the Dutch had regarding their prolific golf ball production. The end of the 16th century saw the city fathers of Delft doing their best to stem the tide of pollution caused by washing the hair used to stuff balls in the city's water supply.

By the 17th century, golf is popping up in references everywhere. Dutch painters themselves seemed to have developed an affinity for the game, as they began traveling to Rome to paint, towing along their clubs and balls! The game even traveled across the Atlantic Ocean, and we know this because of similar ordinances prohibiting the game being played in public places such as Albany, New York, where many Dutch settled. Yet, stick and ball games were not just confined to Europe. There are artistic refer-

Golf art, especially paintings depicting golf's early days, have particular appeal to collectors.

A special rasp for putting fine grooves on wooden faces.

A caddie bag with clubs from 1915–1920.

ences to such games in many cultures, including China, South America and the Pacific Islands dating as far back as the middle ages. What is known is that there are still early records that acknowledge the existence of games very similar to modern golf as far back as the middle ages.

Chole, Jeu de mail, paille maille, pila malleus, etc.

Historians believe that the Roman game of paganica, or pila malleus, was imported to France by Roman soldiers with a fondness for the game. The French version was called paille maille, and the game was played in a court. However, an offshoot of paille maille called jeu de mail a la chicane was born and more closely resembled golf, since it was played along the roads and fields of France, and similarly had trees or doors as the target. Ultimately, jeu de mail made its way to Holland where golf appeared and grew in popularity.

After the battle of Hastings in 1066, in which the noblemen of Flanders gave their support to the victorious William the Conqueror, they were rewarded with extensive land masses in Britain, most notably Lincolnshire and the East Midlands. When an important

Golf cards have become valuable collector's items in recent years.

Flemish widow named Maud was married off to David I of Scotland, the Flemings migrated north to Scotland and took root, becoming an influential and important part of the Court. Descendents of this Flemish family ultimately formed a significant portion of the great nobles of Scotland.

Naturally, the Flemings imported their games of chole or croisse across the English Channel, and many golf historians believe the English game of cambuca was simply the British version of croisse. By the time the game found its way to Scotland, it was probably a version of jeu de mail or croisse. There is no documentation of when these games in Holland may have formed into Scottish golf, but by the 17th century, there are references to Fleming players "holling the ball," so we can be sure it had arrived by then.

Alas, however, the game of golf seems to have died out by the end of the 17th century, and the reason is not entirely clear. Some historians have gone so far as to claim that the 18th century was a more effeminate and refined century, and gentlemen took toward the indoors to pursue such games as billiards. Some historians believe golf was then transformed into or replaced by

Records show that by 1769 there were nearly 200 kolf courts around Amsterdam.

kolf which, in the 18th century, was played in a small enclosed court and under a roof, with walls and a smooth floor similar to a modern gymnasium. The balls ultimately became larger and heavier, and the game is still played in Holland today.

The rules of golf were quite similar to early versions of the French game called mail, and the game became very popular right up to the 19th century. Records show that by 1769 there were nearly 200 kolf courts around and within a short distance of Amsterdam. But although the game of kolf did not die out completely, neither did it merge or transform into the game we know as golf today.

In medieval times, Scotland too had its share of stick and ball games. Once again, ordinances on public record in the 15th century show that the authorities were concerned enough with the more dangerous elements of the game to prohibit or at least curtail "golf-like" activities. On Sundays, and mostly during the winter, townspeople would gather near the church for drinking before and after services, and the entertainment was likely to involve golf and shinty— another stick and ball game which was closely related to golf, but more team oriented.

Bookends from the 1930s.

THE RULES OF GOLF

Since golf seems closely related to the popular Dutch game of golf, it's worth pointing out the rules. The object of the game of golf was to strike a ball with a club toward a target in the distance. Matches were either scored in hole-to-hole accounts with the lowest number of strokes taken per side during match play, or for striking the longest distance for an agreed number of strokes, which was known as flag match. As early as 1500 or so, golfers began to use a hole in the ground as a target, or when playing on ice, a small, painted post. A player would keep score by making a notch in a stick carried by each player.

The rules mandated that a player may use only one club, and generally there were four types of clubs used at the time. The earlier versions of golf consisted of play with all wooden clubs before yielding to forged iron heads since at least the year 1429. Ash and hazel-shafted clubs were then used, and it was common for clubmakers at the time to use personal stamps on the heads, noting the city and name of the manufacturer. Eventually, Scottish cleeks (wooden-headed clubs) imported from Scotland in the early 17th century and made of boxwood weighted with lead, became the club of choice.

The earliest balls used for golf were generally made of boxwood or beechwood before giving way to the more expensive leather balls stuffed with cow's hair. The lower cost of making boxwood balls, however, allowed them to be quite popular among golfers well into the 17th century.

The U.S.G.A. Museum displays scorecards from some of the most dramatic U.S. Opens in history.

BLUSH HILL COUNTRY CLUB

4	3	3	4	4	4	4	4	3	33
267	182	170	373	282	385	353	245	188	2445

										4	3	3	4	4	4	4	4	3	66
4	8	9	3	5	2	1	6	7	2445	267	182	170	373	282	385	353	245	188	2445
2	3	4	5	6	7	8	9												4890
										4	8	9	3	5	2	1	6	7	IN 2445
										10	11	12	13	14	15	16	17	18	

TOTAL 4890 · HANDICAP · NET SCORE

Competition

No. of Hole	Name	Yds.	Stks.	Bogy.	Markr.	Playr.	Bogey Result
1	Hope Grant	440					
2	Nest	280	7	5			
3	The Spinney	176	13	3			
4	Blockade	294	17	3			
5	Heather	394	1	4			
6	Windmill	308	10	4			
7	Elcho	236	15	4			
8	Big Ravine	260	6	4			
9	Long Butt	304	11	4			
Out		2692	36				

SSS 13th Hole 4
SSS Course 71

This Card measures 6 inches diagonally

Replace Turf

	Name	Yds.	Stks.	Bogy.	Markr.	Playr.	Bogey Result
	Running Deer	346	1	4			
	Queensmere	250	16	4			
	Sand Pit	302	9	4			
13	Rise	400	8	5			
14	...ches	284	12	4			
15	Ca...Well	136	18	3			
16	Cæsar's C'mp	316	2	4			
17	Long Hole	460	4	5			
18	Plateau	220	14	3			
In		2714	36				

Gross Score
Less H'cap
Net Score

Date.................195.....
Signed..................

Competition

	SCORE	HOLE	YARDS	PAR
	9	10	324	4
	11	11	314	
		12	437	
			201	
			323	

REPLA...

Hole	Ya...
1	324
2	378
3	123
4	312
5	486
6	260
7	141
8	417
9	325
Total	2766
	35

| | 2690 | | |
| 5380 | 66 | TO... |

HANDICAP
NET SCORE

RE	HOLE	YARDS	PAR	INDEX	SCORE
	10	324	4	10	
	11	314	4	12	
	12	437	4	2	
	13	201	3		
	14	323			
	15	425			
	16	230			
	17	276			
	18	160	3		
		2690	33		
		2690	33	OUT	
		5380	66	TOTAL	
		HANDICAP			
		NET SCORE			

..... Competition.......................................

THE
RISE OF
SCOTTISH
GOLF

The Scottish golf union shield—given to golf clubs that hosted the British Open.

The beginnings of golf in Scotland portray a game that was clearly one of royals, and tracing the history of the game is to understand the bloodlines and rulers of Scotland. For example, we know that in 1457, James II banned "fute-bal" and "Gouff" because the games were distracting the military from its most important archery practice. By 1501, the Treaty of Glasgow was signed, signaling an end to the conflict between Scotland and England. This led to a less strident mandate on archery practice, and ultimately, the ban on golf was no longer enforced.

Perhaps one of the earliest aspiring and ultimately obsessive golfers was the Stuart King, James IV, who seems to have waited patiently for the ban on golf to end before he took up the game with a passion. In fact, there is documentation that the King's High Treasurer was given orders to pay for his Master's "clubs" from a bow-maker in Perth.

Golf was fast becoming the sport of kings, and by the early 1600s, appointments to the Court included the title, "Royal clubmaker." It was common now for Royals to travel to England, with clubs in tow. However, the Court's fondness for the game made it an expensive endeavor for commoners, who were basically shunned from golf. During the nearly two hundred years from the Peace of Glasgow in 1502 to the Revolution in 1688, every single reigning monarch of the Stuart line, which included two kings and one queen of Scotland and four kings of England, played the game of golf.

Perhaps the most legendary anecdote of early golf centers around Mary Stuart, Mary Queen of Scots, who,

Here at St. Andrews, golfers have attempted to break par with everything from long nose woods to titanium drivers.

at her trial in 1586, played golf "in the fields beside Seton" just a few days after the murder of Dranley, her husband. On other occasions, it was known that Mary Queen of Scots played with Mary Seton of Seton Palace, and the two once wagered on a game, with Mary Seton winning a necklace and a Holbein picture.

There are countless other historical references to the royal practice of golf as well. In 1642, Charles I was playing the game at Leith when his noblemen approached with news of the Irish Catholic Rebellion—the beginning of a very troublesome time for the king. There are accounts of this match as well, with one version stating that the king decided to finish off the game. The other, of course, is that Charles was being soundly beaten at the time, and hurried away to avoid having to pay his bet! It is interesting to note that the next account of Charles playing golf finds him a prisoner in the hands of the Scots, playing a game outside the walls of Newcastle-upon-Tyne.

When Charles Edward Stuart, the "Bonnie Prince Charlie" was exiled to Rome after his defeat at Culloden in 1745, he was noted to have relieved his boredom by playing golf in the Borghese Gardens! But the true history of modern golf is generally conceded to have begun in

The early development of golf societies and clubs in Scotland shows the active involvemen of Freemasons.

the mid-18th century with the forming of the first Scottish Golf Clubs. This was significant in that for the first time, there appeared to be a committee or community of golfers to regulate the rules of the game and maintain the courses. It was entirely possible that different communities played golf under different rules and methods of scoring. The game was played on natural grounds, on links courses.

In 1744, we know that The Honourable Company of Edinburgh Golfers was holding meetings, as the first minutes to these gatherings are documented. There is no indication how many meetings may have preceded the 1744 meeting, however, it is generally thought to be, by scholars, the oldest golf club. The purpose of the meeting was to establish a Silver Club competition on the Links of Leith, and the magistrates agreed to provide a trophy. The Silver Club's trophy would be awarded after a tournament similar to an Open Scratch Competition in Edinburgh. The winner would be deemed the "Captain of the Golf" (today it is the Champion Golfer!) and would therefore become something of an arbiter of the game, interpreting rules and generally all matters concerning golf.

Although only ten golfers actually took part in the

The seaside links at St. Andrews have also produced some of the most prolific clubmakers, ncluding Old Tom Morris and Tom Stewart.

tournament, John Rattray, an Edinburgh surgeon, emerged victorious. (He went on to defend his championship the following year.) More importantly, Rattray won the Silver Club itself, the oldest golf trophy in the world.

Ten years later in 1754, twenty-two gentlemen put their signatures on a document to play a championship from the Society of Golfers at St. Andrews. They were men who held golf in high regard as exercise, and though not all of them actually played for the championship, Bailie William Landale, a merchant in St. Andrews was the winner. In this tournament, however, the winner did not become Captain of Golf, but rather simply the winner of a local golf championship. This was the beginning of the Royal and Ancient Golf Club of St. Andrews.

The early development of golf societies and clubs in Scotland shows the active involvement of Freemasons. Although competition was intended to be open to all golfers, it was soon apparent that these clubs were designating the competition only for St. Andrews Gentlemen and Gentlemen at Leith. In effect, a closed competition. Politically, the City of St. Andrews had demonstrated some Jacobite leanings, and Scottish Masonic golfers are believed to have formed secret "clubs within a club" and the Freemasons took pains to keep the game private. In fact, it is generally conceded that golf may not have actually survived without the

secrecy and thoroughness in which the Freemasons regulated the game of golf.

By 1853, the Union Club of St. Andrews agreed to build a new clubhouse for its archers, and also accommodate golfers as well. Although they were housed under the same clubhouse, the Union Club and the Royal and Ancient Golf Club of St. Andrews maintained separate identities. By 1877, the golfing membership had enjoyed a significant increase in members, and archery began to subside. It was in May of that year that the two clubs agreed to merge. It was no doubt attributed to the influence of the Freemasons that archers and golfers shared a common clubhouse, and the two "sports" are linked tightly in Scottish history.

Although competition for the Silver Club generated a certain amount of public interest, it dimmed in comparison to the excitement generated by a high-stakes match between well-known amateurs. Betting was common, and in a match between two golfers of equal skill, it was more likely that, instead of handicapping by conceding strokes during a round, odds were put into place. Eventually, the revered age of private match play games was basically done away with by the implementation of the first Championships in the middle 1800s.

On April 6th, 1857, members of the Prestwick Club sent a letter out proposing a match between the eight

From Old Tom Morris to Tiger Woods, many of the greatest names in golf have crossed the stone bridge over Swilcan Burn on the Old Course at St. Andrews on their way to victory.

prominent golf clubs. The match would be comprised of the best four golfers from each club, with the game to be played in double matches or foursomes drawn randomly. The winning pair would be awarded a medal, and they would compete against each other in a single match, the winner's club to become the possessor of the medal.

The Prestwick letter was such a success that four other clubs asked to join in the competition, and it was determined that the matches would be held at St. Andrews, with the winner receiving a silver claret jug. In the end, the Royal Blackheath Golf Club trounced The Royal and Ancient St. Andrews Golf Club. The following year, the Claret Jug would be awarded to a single golfer rather than a club, and were it not for a heated rivalry between Willie Park and Old Tom Morris, the Championship may have faded. In the first eight singles competitions, Morris would win four Championships to Park's three.

Old Tom Morris spent his early years as a clubmaker's apprentice, and in 1851, he became the custodian of the Prestwick Club's links course. Playing out of Prestwick, Morris established himself as the best golfer in the world, and he was ultimately hired (after repeated pleas on the part of the R & A) to be head greenskeeper at St.

Scottish links golf was aesthetically pleasing, infinitely challenging, and perhaps most importantly, easy to maintain.

Andrews—a position he held for forty years.

His fame, however, owes more to his spirit as a presence at St. Andrews rather than his accomplishments on the golf course. One of the pioneering Scots of professional golf, Morris was not only regarded as the first of the great players, but a character and institution. He retired in 1904, but held the honorary position for four more years until his death. Old Tom Morris' funeral was a day of mourning in St. Andrews, and his reputation and spirit continue to linger in the game today. His pro shop beside the 18th green, as well as his portrait, which hangs inside the clubhouse, help to immortalize the man and his influence on the game of golf.

Great Old Tom Morris was an extraordinary player, but it is universally acknowledged that his son, Young Tom Morris, reached an even higher plateau. At the age of 16, Young Tom won a big tournament at Carnoustie from a top level professional after winning a playoff with Willie Park and Bob Andrew, another elite player from Perth. That same year, Young Tom finished fourth in the Open Championship, but the next year he began a string of four straight championships which has not been equaled yet. Most impressive is the fact that Young Tom didn't just emerge victorious in these Championships,

A #4 iron from the 1860s, from the Geo Nicoll Leven Club in Scotland.

rather he won them in convincing fashion, by as many as 12 strokes over his contemporaries in 36 hole contests.

Young Tom was so strong a player that his scoring records were never equaled while in the gutta percha ball era. Sadly, Young Tom was just finishing a match in 1875 when he received a telegram that his wife and new-born baby were very ill. He was just about to board a boat to return home when he received another message that his wife and baby had died. It was said that the great golfer never recovered from this tragedy, and he died of a broken heart on Christmas Day that same year.

Eventually, the St. Andrews Club superseded the

Honourable Company as the true arbiter and overseer of the game of golf. The quality of the turf at St. Andrews, along with the quality of golfers and the beauty of the course itself, was the reason more and more golf clubs turned to the R & A for leadership. It didn't hurt that the older Honourable Company changed its site and lost ground to St. Andrews as well. In 1897, the Royal and Ancient club agreed to become the governing authority on the rules of the game. But one could not count out the impact both Young and Old Tom Morris had on the game of golf at St. Andrews. The charm and spirit of these two men continue to add mystique to the Old Course today,

Left to right:

Noted St. Andrews clubmaker Tom Stewart designed this iron pre-1900.

Scottish clubs were the choice for many professional golfers around the turn of the 20th century.

Spalding made clubs in Scotland, such as this iron from the late 1800s.

as thousands of golfers across the world visit the "Home of Golf" each year.

Many theories abound as to why golf took hold in Scotland with such passion. One reason is as clear as day. The country's beautiful coastlines seem to be made for the game. In lowland parts of Scotland, the "links" between the beach and land that is ripe for farming are hilly grassland areas where nature created seemingly perfect hazards and fairways. The term "links" is derived from the Scottish word *lynk's*, meaning "ridges, hummocks" and also "rough open ground." In general, it referred to a tract of low-lying seaside land on the east coast of the Lowlands which was held by a town and used during the Middle Ages for sports such as archery and golf. The land is characteristically sandy and treeless, with undulating turf, wind-swept dunes and natural pot bunkers. The turf was typically comprised of bent grass, with gorse bushes quite prevalent.

In short, the land must have tantalized and tortured the country's earliest golfers. The grassy areas were kept short by nature's natural greens keepers—Scotland's grazing animals, creating near perfect links fairways. The growth of fescue throughout the links land also provided a natural penalty for golfers who missed the short grass.

Scottish links golf was esthetically pleasing, infinitely challenging and perhaps most importantly, easy to maintain. Yet, Ireland and Britain also have similar landscapes that are ideal for golf, and the game was being played in both countries around the same time golf reached Scotland. So clearly, the land alone did not enable Scotland to make the undisputed claim of being the home of golf. For that to happen, it is important to look not to the land, but the people of Scotland.

While forms of golf died out in other parts of the world, such as Holland and France, the intractable, hard-headed Freemasons of Scotland, despite their secret, closed societies, stubbornly kept the game alive, and indeed, enabled it to take root into the popular world game that it is today.

Early golf societies took great pride and careful measures to preserve the game they so boldly took claim to, while golf and other forms of the game simply transformed into other games (such as kolf in Holland) or faded away completely.

Mallot and center shafted putters were once banned by the Royal and Ancient Golf Club.

THE AGRIPPA
GOLF BALL COMPᴾʸ

VENTRY

Thoroughly
Seasoned

"Woodley Flier"

GOLF BALLS

TRIANON
MILLS

"Woodley Flier" Embossed on every ball.
Guaranteed made from new material.

EARLY
GOLF BALLS

Golf ball boxes from 1890–1900.

THE BOXWOOD

Trying to determine the exact origins and characteristics of the boxwood ball is a bit like trying to pinpoint the precise moment in time when the game of golf began. The earliest golfers are said to have played the game with a hardwood ball very similar in nature to the balls used in pall mall and chole in England and Belgium respectively.

Believed to be made of beech or boxroot, these hardwood balls were handcrafted on a carpenter's lathe in many estimates, between the 13th and 17th centuries. While the balls were not very sophisticated and tended to indent, split and become misshapen during the course of the game, they were balls that were inexpensive to construct and generally permitted common folks to play. For this reason, they remained popular for centuries of play, despite advances in ballmaking.

Another downside to the boxwood ball is that it had a tendency to stray dramatically if not struck cleanly by a club. Wild, hardwood projectiles naturally led to broken windows and worse, injuries to those in the general vicinity. However, the upside was that in the early 14th century, medieval laws began to appear on the books in prohibiting the playing of certain "stick and ball" games in areas that were more populated, thus enabling historians to track and date the origins of the game.

THE FEATHERY

There is also a bit of uncertainty as to when the feather ball period of golf truly began, given what we know of the paganica in ancient Roman times. Some historians suspect the ball may have been around Europe and used in golf-like games as early as the 1400s, while others believe it wasn't until 200 years later when the ball was introduced. What is clear is that because of the more expensive nature of the feather ball's construction, the game of golf stopped expanding in the early 1800s.

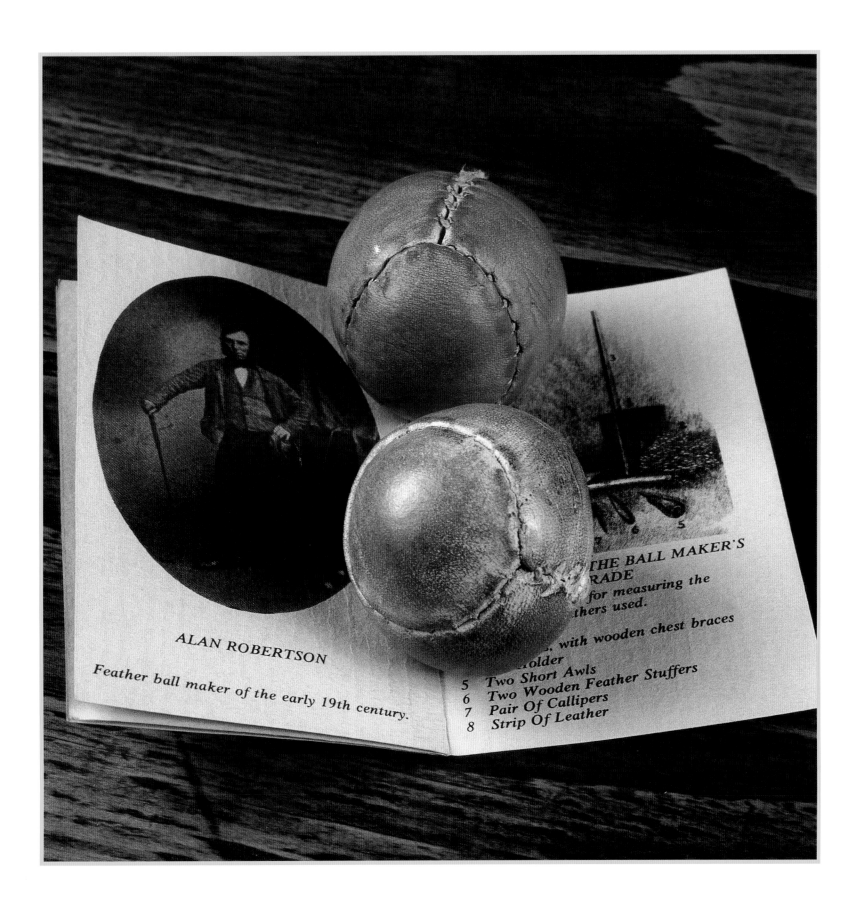

ALAN ROBERTSON

Feather ball maker of the early 19th century.

THE BALL MAKER'S
TRADE

for measuring the
thers used.

with wooden chest braces

older
5 Two Short Awls
6 Two Wooden Feather Stuffers
7 Pair Of Callipers
8 Strip Of Leather

Feather balls.

A century earlier, the cheap boxwood ball enabled the game to spread to the masses. But in the early 17th century, the feathery began to gain in popularity. Here was a ball that required more finesse than power and rewarded the cleanly struck shot rather than brutal strength. However, the ball was much more expensive to make and it had a lasting effect on the game. Golf became a sport only for the wealthy and privileged because they were the only ones who could afford to pay for the feather ball.

Not only were the feather balls expensive to make, but the average golfer was not likely to finish a round using just one. The earliest feather balls were actually leather cased balls stuffed with wool or hair. In most cases, these balls had three pieces of leather about $\frac{1}{16}$ inch thick and made of either bull or horse hide.

Two end pieces (often soaked in alum water) were joined together by a rectangular middle piece— $\frac{5}{32}$ of an inch thick leather flap. The flap had tiny holes perforating it, enabling twine stitching to form a hollow case, and the pouch was simply turned inside-out through a small hole that was used for the stuffing of the ball.

This inside-out turning of the casing protected the wax twine under the edge of the leather cover. Then, the case was stuffed very tight (using a "brogue," a blunt-edged iron spike) with either chicken breast feathers or wet goose down and stitched shut with twine. More important to the ball's performance was the manner in which the ball was prepared after it was stuffed. The wet leather would ultimately shrink once it dried, thus tightening around the feathers, which actually expanded when they became dry.

The result of these two opposing factors eventually produced a very hard, fairly resilient ball, which was hammered round by the ballmaker and then painted to add further protection from the elements.

The ball was capable of flying 200 yards in the air by better players, but more importantly, it proved to be very workable. Finesse ball strikers were able to control it and the game of golf was reaching a new stage in its evolution. Ballmaking was becoming an art.

But the feathery was not without its problems, cost being the most noticeable. The best ballmakers were incapable of making more than four a day, and it was generally assumed that anyone making more than that in a single day was simply not making a ball worth owning. Featheries cost more than ten times what the old boxwood balls cost, and adding insult to injury, they weren't nearly as durable.

In spite of its resilience and the golfer's ability to have more control over the direction and trajectory of the feathery, even the finest golfers were unable to avoid water from time to time. Even though featheries would

A long nose spoon with feather ball.

float and it would take days of exposure to water to saturate, a waterlogged feathery would often come out of play until the leather cover had time to dry and be treated again. But that was the least of a golfer's problem. Skull an iron shot with a wet feathery ball and there was a good chance the stuffing would be knocked out of it. Therefore, even a decent player would have to carry a half-dozen featheries in his bag for a round of golf.

The expense of the feathery ball naturally produced varied quality in the balls produced. There does not appear to be any standardization of the size or weight of a feathery ball, but most seemed to be about 1.6 inches in diameter, which is close to what today's balls measure. Feather balls were usually about 1.5 ounces, but ballmakers varied the weight by the method in which they stuffed them. A golfer might prefer a lighter ball, say 1.32 ounces, for downwind shots, and a heavier ball closer to 2 ounces when playing into the wind. (The rules of golf in the early 1800s permitted the golfer to change balls at the start of a new hole.)

Ballmakers also made different grades of balls—the highest quality balls, and culls, which were generally sorted out because they weren't perfectly stuffed or had some kind of stitching flaw. As a result, culls were often used as practice or range balls, or maybe carried deep in a golfer's bag for those days when his swing was not in

sync and he didn't want to risk skulling a shot on a good ball before finishing his round.

A good player could make a feathery last for many holes by striking it cleanly on the harder sides. After time, though, the ball would soften and ultimately become unplayable. What many don't realize is that the feathery was never really round. In fact, the looser stuffed balls were more round than the properly packed featheries. Yet, despite their oblong characteristics, featheries did fly and roll quite true on the courses of the day.

THE GUTTA PERCHA

While the introduction of the expensive feathery was unable to render obsolete the boxwood ball, (and nearly the game of golf itself) the invention of the Gutta Percha golf ball in the early 1850s soon established the featheries as collectors' items. For the game to survive, a ball would have to come along that would be cheaper, less vulnerable to the elements, more durable and yet workable for the finesse player. Round would be nice, too.

The Gutta Percha accomplished just that. Arriving from East Asia in around 1848, the ball enjoyed over 50 years of prosperity and managed to attract more people to the game of golf because of its affordability. No longer was golf merely a game for the wealthy and royal.

The exact origin of the Gutta Percha is not clearly

An autographed golf ball by Bobby Jones from one of his four U.S. Open victories.

defined. One disputed, albeit romantic saga revolves around the Reverend James Paterson of Dundee who, it is claimed, made the first Gutta Percha ball in 1845. Paterson, a Scottish missionary working in India shipped a Hindu statue to his brother, Robert, a ministry student back home in St. Andrews. Inside the crate used to ship the statue were chunks of rubbery gutta percha used as packing material, which Robert attempted to resole his boots with. At some point, he gave up on the boots, but then tried to make a golf ball, which he took to the Old Course in April 1845 for a test round. He either liked what he found, or gave up on the idea completely, because a third Paterson brother who lived near Edinburgh began manufacturing gutta percha balls. Under the name of "Paterson's Patent" the gutty ball was originally made to resemble the feathery, with a smooth surface and lines engraved to mimic the seams on feathery balls.

Made from the dried sap of sapodilla trees of East Asia, the substance was sent to Scotland in sheets, which ballmakers then cut into patches or strips, softened them in hot water, and rounded them by hand into a ball. Once the desired shape and size was achieved, the balls were then dipped into cold water for hardening.

Soon after Paterson, other Scots joined in the gutta percha movement. While some golf "purists" argued that featheries were the superior ball, transition to the gutty

was fairly swift and unanimous, making it the standard equipment of play. Still, the first gutties were not without their own set of problems.

Smooth as marbles or billiard balls, gutties had little aerodynamic stability. They tended not to get airborn with much consistency, and would often dive or bore down in flight. In fact, some professionals became so disappointed with the poor performance and trajectories of the gutties that they gave them away, often to their caddies to play. Not long after that, professionals noticed their caddies were achieving the kind of ball flight they themselves desired with beat up, secondhand gutta balls.

So it was quite by accident that an experiment with physics and aerodynamics led to the second generation in gutta percha golf ball design. Players noticed that the nicks and scratches on the surface of the ball caused a truer, more stable trajectory. Robert Forgan, a club and ballmaker from St. Andrews is credited with selling the first gutta percha balls with surface patterns. Forgan placed each ball in a mount and indented the surface with the claw end of the hammer, attempting to simulate cuts and scratches made by a golf club. For twenty years to follow, Forgan's method became the standard on gutta balls, and the practice became known as "hand hammered."

Now golfers had a ball that traveled further, rolled more consistently, and was significantly less expensive to

"THE DEVELOPMENT OF THE GOLF BALL"

WOODEN	FEATHERY	GUTTA PERCHA	MACHINE GUTTY	HASKELL
c.1590	c.1790	c.1850	c.1880	c.1900

The evolution of the golf ball dramatically changed
the shape and design of golf clubs as well.

make than the feathery. People were coming back to golf in droves and the game enjoyed a rebirth among the common people. Forests in Asia were being gutted to satisfy the demand for the new gutta percha ball, and ballmakers were able to significantly increase their production of golf balls.

As a result, golf began to grow at a rapid rate outside of Great Britain. Toward the end of the 19th century, markings on the gutta ball were being applied in the mold, with the earliest patterns appearing to be circular marks emanating from the poles of the ball. Experimentation was now the rage, and manufacturers continued to design, redesign and create molds, all promising improved ball flight. The amount of unique pattern designs is actually what makes the gutty ball the sought after collectibles that they are today. One can find circles and triangles among the many geometric shapes that were used as marking patterns for these balls at some time in their history.

One of the most well known balls to emerge from the gutta percha period was the A. G. Spalding & Bros. Vardon Flyer, which Harry Vardon, the soft-spoken Englishman who, many believe, took the golf craze in America to new levels during his nine month tour of the States in 1900.

The process of making featheries was an art form. Ballmakers would take over three hours to make a single ball, and a mistake could cost them half their day. If you were a maker of featheries, you didn't have much time to learn the art of clubmaking. However, once gutties became the golf ball of desire, clubmakers easily shifted into ballmaking mode by purchasing molds and substantially increasing their incomes by meeting the demand for gutties.

Gutties were not without their share of problems, though. In cold weather, the gutta percha could become brittle and when struck, actually break apart. This problem was even addressed in the rules at the time. If a gutty ball broke, a player was allowed to drop another in the spot next to the largest remaining piece of the broken ball.

In hot weather, the gutty could become soft, lose it's compression and not fly nearly as far as it would in mild weather. Still, none of these problems were enough to send the golf world scurrying back to featheries.

Before long, every serious clubmaker had his own brand of gutty ball, and by the end of the century, there were hundreds of brands on the market, creating the kind of competition for market share that golf enjoys today. Collectors also benefit from the variety of gutties manufactured then.

The gutta percha ball ranged in weight from about 1.4 ounces to 1.7 ounces. The average guttie traveled about 30 yards farther than the feathery, and because of it's stability, tended to last much longer as well. When

Golf ball molds with golf ball, 1880–1900.

struck, the gutta percha generally made a clicking noise at impact. Aged gutties are often dark brown and nearly black, but sound and color are not enough to tell if a ball is pure gutty, as some early rubber core balls often had a gutta percha cover.

Collectors of gutta percha balls will often come across balls that were remade, or with several layers of enamel and paint. This was a common way gutties further brought golf to the masses. Old balls found or purchased from golfers were remade and resold back into the market. And while finding a retouched gutty generally doesn't diminish the collectibility of the item, there are few things more scarce than finding a gutty with its original paint and markings intact.

THE RUBBER CORE OR MODERN BALL

By the time Harry Vardon returned to England after his whirlwind tour of the states, his Vardon Flyer was quickly becoming obsolete. A few years before Vardon arrived in America, an entrepreneur from Cleveland, Ohio was thinking of ways to improve his own game. The shortest hitter in his foursome, Coburn Haskell happened to be visiting a friend of his at the B.F. Goodrich rubber company in Akron when he discovered some elastic threads of rubber sitting in a bin. He returned home with the strips and attempted to wind them into a ball, but his early attempts would often end in frustration as the ball would slip from his hands and unwind furiously as Haskell chased it around the room.

Eventually, Haskell persuaded Goodrich to help him find a way to wrap the balls with high tension and put a gutta percha cover around the wound rubber ball. It would ultimately become America's greatest contribution to the game of golf. The Haskell ball immediately flew a good 25 yards further than the gutta percha ball in the air, and it rolled even further than the gutties.

The first Haskell balls were a bit wild. Nicknamed "Bounding Billy's" by players, these early balls virtually exploded on impact because of irregularities in the winding process. The balls did not land on greens as softly as the gutties, and ballmakers began to experiment with the thickness of the gutta percha covers in an attempt to solve some of the Haskell's trajectory inconsistencies.

By the turn of the century, molded covers quickly yielded to raised, round nubs of the bramble pattern, and a thicker gutta cover was becoming the norm. This helped to reduce the "jacked-up" liveliness of the ball.

Accordingly, the game of golf began to change as dramatically as the ball itself. The added distance most golfers enjoyed with the new Haskell balls completely altered the strategy players used on the course. Par fives were reduced to par fours in many cases, and balls that

A Willie Park mid-iron from 1886, as well as two feathery balls from 1850, and two dimpled rubber-core balls from 1940–1950.

no longer landed softly on the greens led to the increased employment of bump and run shots.

As might be expected, there was a great deal of resistance to the Haskell ball, especially in Europe. Prominent British golfers urged fellow professionals not to use the ball, describing it as unfit, and even unmanly because of the added distance. But in a game where everyone is constantly searching for the slightest advantage over their opponents, it wasn't long before even the most vocal critics of the ball had to eventually accept the fact that the Haskell ball was here to stay and there would be no turning back. The modern ball had a very deep impact on the game, most noticeably the clubs. Although golf courses themselves were altered and strategies rethought, the actual tools used to strike the rubber core balls were the most dramatic. At first, rubber core balls were more expensive to produce than the gutta percha balls, but once free market competition emerged, the costs were greatly reduced.

It is interesting to note that the first golf ball patent (No. 3428) was issued in England in 1876 to a Captain Duncan Stewart of St. Andrew's, Scotland, who invented a ball that combined gutta percha with cork and metal fillings in an effort to prevent the ball from splitting open. The ball Stewart attempted to develop was not successful, but he persisted with various other rubber threads within a gutta percha cover.

In 1905, Stewart testified in the defense of a patent violation case where the Haskell Company sued British ball manufacturers for developing their own rubber core balls. Stewart's testimony about his own experiments ultimately enabled the British to void the Haskell patent in the UK.

In 1907, an English engineer by the name of William Tyler was given a patent for developing a dimple-covered golf ball, which the A.G. Spalding & Bros. company purchased U.S. rights to. The next year, Spalding began to produce dimple covered balls until 1912, when mesh and lattice (square or fishnet) became the pattern most golfers favored, and they lasted well into the 1930s.

The early 1900s saw a great deal of experimentation with golf balls. Frank H. Mingay of Berfield, Scotland was given a British patent for his use of incompressible liquid centered golf balls. Mingay used water, treacle, castor oil, honey and even mercury in his research, hoping to invent the ball which would receive and transmit clubhead impact energy at a minimal loss of total energy. Again, A.G. Spalding stepped in to purchase the rights to Mingay's patent and ultimately introduced the "Witch," Spalding's first liquid center golf ball. By that time, however, the "Witch" was but one of several liquid center balls already available to golfers.

In 1931, the United States Golf Association recog-

Winged Foot imprinted balls, along with various antique clubs, including the Schenectady putter.

nized that the advances in ball design needed to be regulated, and ruled that no ball weighing more than 1.55 ounces or smaller than 1.68" in diameter could be played in their championships. While Americans did not seem to mind much, players from England and Scotland did not take much comfort in this ruling. Links golf was a different game, they argued, and with the heavy winds they were accustomed to, a smaller and heavier ball was needed. After much back and forth, the USGA and the Royal and Ancient Golf Association reached a compromise.

Beginning on the first day of 1932, the R & A set their measurements—an official 1.62 ounces was maximum while 1.62 inches for a diameter was now the rule for a ball. The USGA agreed with the 1.62 ounce maximum weight, but maintained 1.68 inch as the minimum diameter of a ball. Ballmakers since then have attempted to improve performance by experimenting in several areas, while still maintaining approved status by the USGA. Balata balls, wound balls, two piece and three-piece balls, and liquid center balls have all come into fashion since.

Another important development was the implementation of a surlyn cover which proved to be more durable than balata. Surlyn balls last longer, generally don't lose their shape, or suffer disfiguring cuts from bad swings or skulled shots, and even cost less to produce. Many surlyn balls are often designed to impart low spin rates, lessening slices and hooks—another factor that has helped make golf more enjoyable for the high handicapper.

Olin Dutra, fighting severe stomach cramps, won the 1934 U.S. Open at the Merion Cricket Club in Ardmore, Pennsylvania, using this ball.

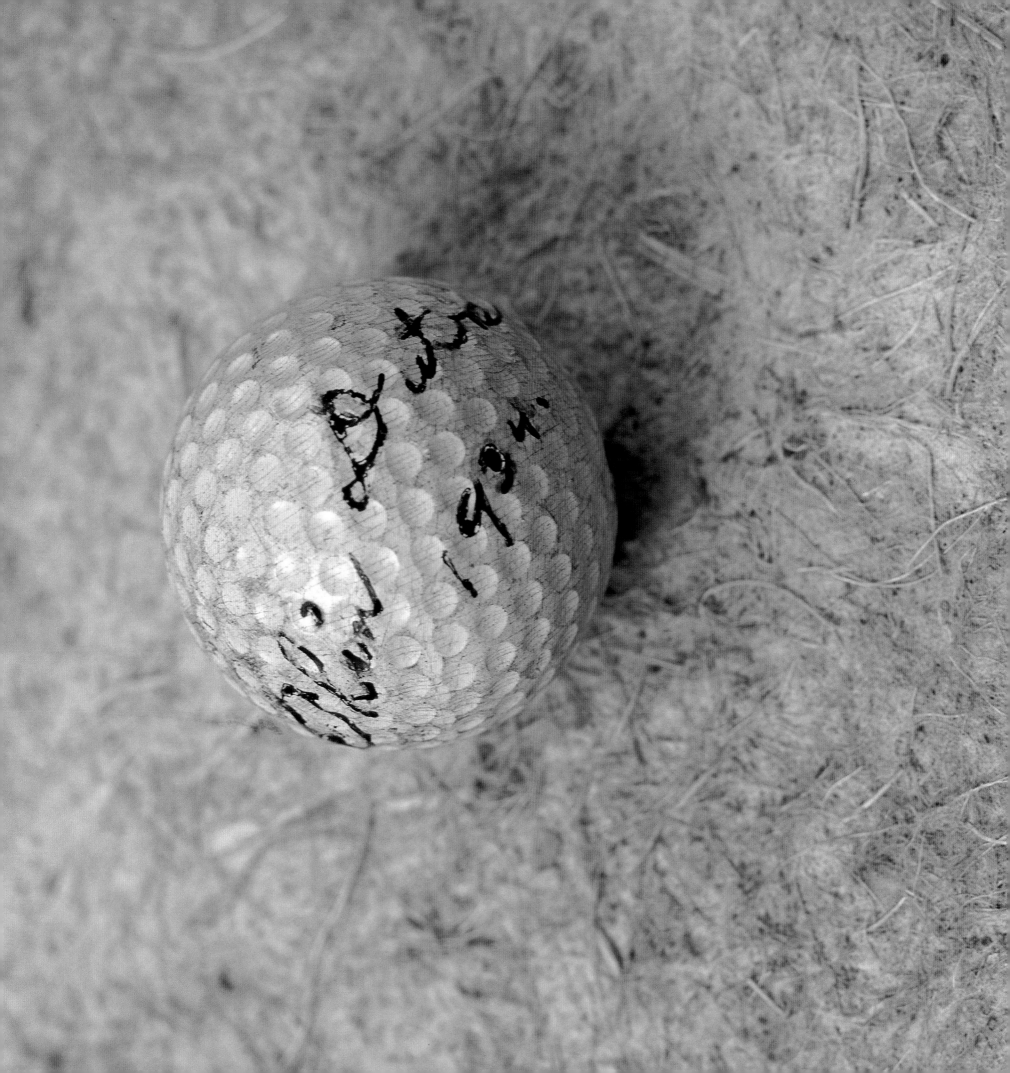

EARLY
GOLF CLUBS

Various antique putters.

THE WOODS

It is telling that, in terms of golf club invention, the iron clubhead is a relative newcomer to golf. Golf historians generally believe that wood clubs preceded irons by centuries. How many centuries is still a topic of debate, since the origin of the game of golf has never been proven. There is an old myth of golf being invented by the shepherd boy who, passing time while minding his sheep, hits a stone with his staff, only to see the stone drop into a distant hole. No one knows if that myth has any truth to it, and it doesn't seem too far fetched to be possible. But one thing is for sure. The shepherd boy was probably not hitting an iron.

The oldest documented golf clubs, unfortunately, can only be found in old paintings and descriptions from centuries ago. However, Sotheby's, the noted auction house, sold a club in 1992 for over $150,000 which is currently displayed in the museum in Spain's famed Valderrama Golf Club. And it is with a touch of irony that this old club is an iron! Historians date the club to about 1680, and it was found centuries later in a shed in Edinburgh and well kept by its owner. Leave it to a Scotsman to be astute enough to wrap the club in a cloth soaked with linseed oil for over 40 years, for the club is in excellent condition today.

One of the problems historians and collectors are faced with is the deterioration of wood over time. Unless effort was made over time to preserve wooden clubs, they simply disappeared, which explains the prevalence of early irons.

Among the oldest clubs in existence are the "Troon Clubs" which were found inside a boarded-up closet, along with a newspaper dated 1741. It turned out the clubs were actually much older than the newspaper. Some golf historians estimate the Troon Clubs were made in the early 1600s, and quite possibly the 15th cen-

Long nose woods from 1850–1900.

tury. The clubs are comprised of six long nose woods (drivers and spoons) and two irons. Determining the exact age of golf clubs prior to the mid 19th century is quite difficult since the markings clubmakers often stamped on clubs cannot be documented or attributed to specific craftsmen so far back in time. The Troon clubs are very valuable in that they add a great deal of perspective toward the dating of other early clubs.

Long Nose Woods and Spoons

Since feathery balls were susceptible to damage from a poorly hit iron, the clubs of choice in the feathery era were long nose woods and spoons. With long, slim heads, a concave face and shallow clubfaces, the long nosed woods were characterized according to the desired shot. It was not uncommon for a player to carry with him eight to twelve clubs, including two "play clubs", a grassed driver, three or more spoons, a baffy spoon, a wooden niblick and a wooden putter.

Prior to the mid 1880s, a golfer standing on the first tee would be very likely to hit with his play club which was the driver of the era. With a long shaft and low loft, the play club was the club of choice for hitting the ball the greatest distance possible. Another long nosed wood that was quite useful was the "grassed driver" which had more loft than play clubs and helped the golfer get the ball in the air. The grassed driver was used from the tee as well as the fairway, but it would still require a good lie from the short grass.

Instead of having irons that ranged from long to mid to wedges the way a golfer today does, the 19th century golfer was mostly likely to employ either a "long spoon," a "middle spoon," a "short spoon" or a "baffy spoon" depending upon his distance from the green. Long spoons generally had longer shafts than middle spoons, even though the middle spoon might be stiffer in shaft flexibility. Short spoons and baffy spoons had more loft to them.

The baffy spoon was early golf's version of the wedge, as it was often employed to achieve a high trajectory over a hazard, and to land softly on the green with minimum roll. Collectors note that the baffing or baffy spoon are more rare, as long nose era golfers began to move toward the iron lofter instead. Even more difficult to come across are the wooden niblicks from the latter part of the 19th century. Used to advance the ball from out of a trouble spot, the wooden niblick features a smaller, but heavily lofted clubface. These clubs never achieved the durability of other long nosed woods and were ultimately replaced by irons.

Historians believe that the Scottish clubs of the 15th century were remarkably similar in design to the clubs a player might carry today, with the exception of the tech-

Mixture of play clubs, including spoons and grass drivers.

nology and the adjustments to the modern ball. A typical 15th century club had a very sturdy shaft, a weighted head and a handle gripped with hide from a pig, sheep, cow or horse. A chamois grip might also have been a possibility.

When the long nosed woods came into fashion in the 18th century, golfers typically used a flatter swing to advance the ball with a low trajectory but a great distance because of roll. But play clubs were also likely to crack or split upon impact, the reason why many golfers of that period usually carried a couple of play clubs.

These early woods were made from a sturdy, straight-grained shaft which tapered to a long flat wedge. The wedge was then joined to a taper on the socket of the clubhead and glued before finally being held into place by tightly wrapped twine around the tapering splice in a process known as "whipping." There was a great deal of variation in the choice of wood used to make these clubs. Clubmakers generally preferred to use the fruitwoods, such as apple, pear, cherry and plum to make long nose heads, as well as dogwood, hornbeam, thornwood and beech. Whatever the wood, it was important for the clubhead to have the grain running up the neck of the club so as to limit its vulnerability to splitting upon impact with a golf ball. This was accomplished best by having a natural bend in the wood.

The earliest form of wood used in a clubhead was the "thorncut" which was made of wood from a blackthorn tree. It was apparently important to have the grain running up the neck of the clubface, so the manner in which the blackthorn tree was cut (with wedges to make a stronger piece of wood) appears to have been vital. Cut this way, the blackthorn was less likely to split upon impact with a golf ball. Therefore, putting a natural bend into the clubface was highly desirable.

Beech was also a popular wood for clubheads, and the quality of this wood was used until the turn of the 20th century. Clubmakers were careful with beech, choosing only from trees that grew on hills rather than in the valley.

The reason—valley wood had a tendency to be softer. Along the way, other woods were tried, such as apple, dogwood and holly, but beech appeared to be the most popular choice among early clubmakers.

For about the first 400 years or so of the game's development, wooden clubheads were joined to a shaft in roughly the same manner. That is, basically strapping the shaft to the back of the head in a flat join which would be glued and then whipped with twine. The twine was generally used to either conceal the join at the head and shaft, or to add strength to the joining. Twine was simply flax derived from the linseed plant and covered with hot pitch to protect it.

Some clubmakers, in an attempt to avoid having to

*The development of modern woods. From left to right, a modern Persimmon with brass insert
made by Wheatley Golf, a MacGregor Jack Nicklaus driver, and a Taylor Made metal wood from 1987.*

fasten a clubhead to a shaft, experimented with a one-piece club. But they never became as popular as separate woods for both clubhead and shaft. One problem was that once a one piece club was broken, there was no chance to fix it. Most of the breaks from clubs prior to the one-piece were centered in the area where the shaft and clubhead were joined, and this was not an uncommon occurrence in a round of golf. There was simply no way to reshaft a one-piece club. It wasn't until nearly the beginning of the 19th century when splice fixing became the preferred method of linking the shaft and the clubhead.

Early long nose woods were heavy, and designed to swing through the long grass that the golfer of the times often encountered. It was also not uncommon for a club-maker to fasten lead as a backweight on long nosed woods prior to the 1800s. The earliest clubmakers were often bowmakers and carpenters who already had a fine understanding, passed down from generations of bow-makers and carpenters before them, of the different qualities of wood. Before the arrival of machine tools, clubmakers prior to the late 1800s had to make clubs by hand. A playclub would be made by forming a block of wood into a shaped head with a curved socket which would taper into a splice so that it could be fitted to the shaft. The process would generally involve filing, spoke-shaving, and chiseling, before the club was leaded,

boned, glasspapered down to the require length, usually stained with a keel (red keel was a popular finish) and ultimately treated with a hare's foot dipped in a mixture of oil and varnish.

The tools used for this work would be the usual tools of any woodworking craftsman of the time might use, namely hammers, saws, files, planes and drills. A club-maker would also use a Bunsen burner to melt lead, which was then ladled into a groove on the back of the club to provide the desired weight and balance.

The earliest long nosed woods are long and shallow faced with a slight hook or spoon bend to them. In clubs made before 1860 or so, there do not appear to be any with a face deeper than an inch on play clubs. Only in baffing spoons and other, more lofted clubs does the face exceed an inch or so in deepness.

Ultimately, the demand for golf clubs became so great that there became a need for specialization. Clubmakers were often men who were employed at specific golf courses as rangers or supervisors. They may have regulated play, repaired members' clubs, maintained the course and even play the game. In short, the game was becoming more popular and bowmakers were no longer the men golfers turned to for quality golf clubs.

Many times, ram's horn (or ramshorn) was used as an insert in the sole or face of the club to reduce damage

Photographic portrait of a golfer.

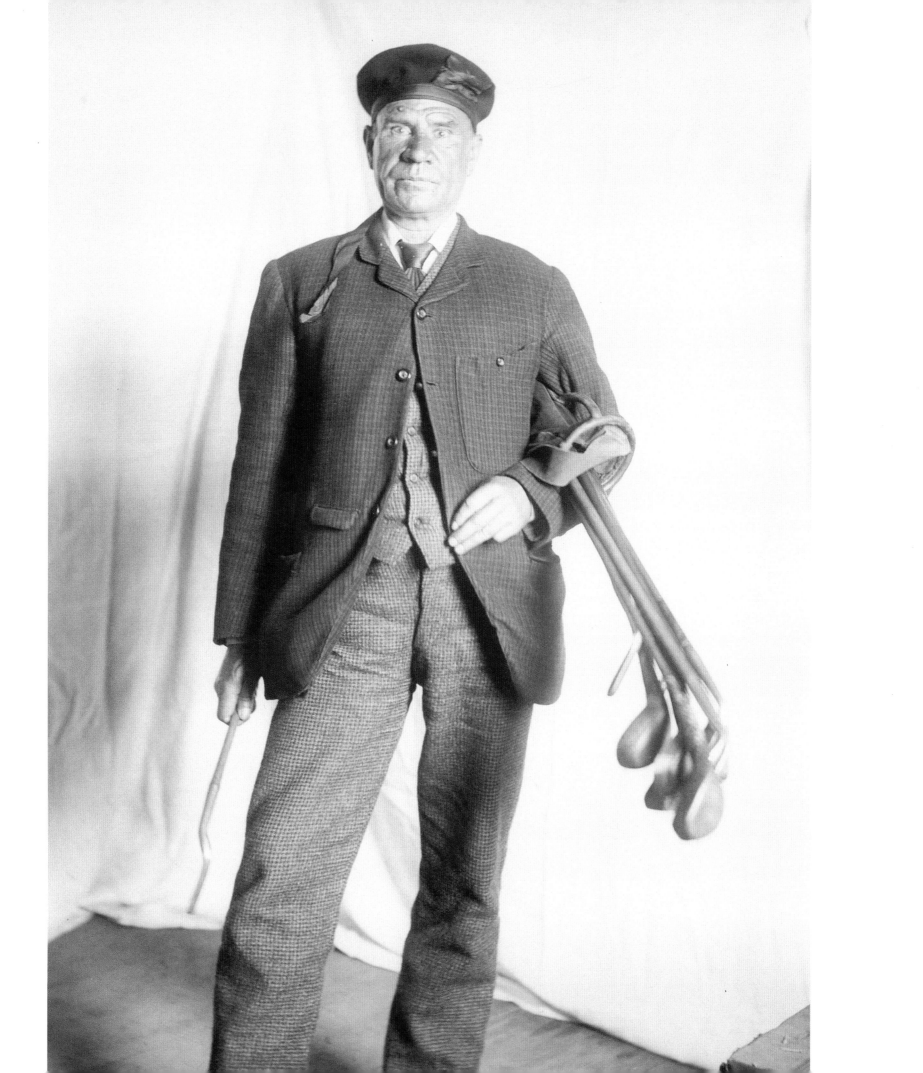

done to the clubs by struck rocks and stones in the course of a player's swing. These plates were made by cutting the horn of either a ram or cow, then softening the pieces by boiling them in water. The softened horn was then made flat by squeezing it in a vice. The plate was then inserted into the sole, fastened with pegs, and could be easily replaced when worn.

Another way of protecting and adding weight to a clubhead was by heating lead, then pouring the molten liquid into a cavity placed in the back of the clubhead. Soft lead was generally used for this process, and when poured down the cavities, the lead would become solid again. This was also another way a clubmaker could customize a club, weighing it differently to alter its swing characteristics. Fixing a soleplate to a clubhead was another important step that a clubmaker would take to both protect the wood and add weight to the club. Most of the early woods featured a brass soleplate, fixed to the club with brass screws.

Early golf grips were usually made of sheepskin or cowhide and were obtained from a sheet of leather cut with a chisel. Before a grip was fastened, it was likely that an undergrip of cloth, called "listings" was applied so that the leather grip would adhere better to the club. This also resulted in a much thicker grip.

Early clubmakers used keratin, a mixture of sheep and cattle horn and hooves, which, when crushed and heated, formed a natural fixative. It was very effective, unless it became wet, so the whipping process with twine was more than just decorative. It served to protect the glue.

Eventually, clubmakers found persimmon, a dense and straight-grained wood that was imported to Scotland from North American forests. The quality of persimmon woods was so great that persimmon became the wood of choice deep into the modern era of golf.

Shafts

In the late 17th century, it is generally believed that hazel was a popular choice of wood for a club's shaft. Scholars have noted that hazel would have made a rather whippy shaft, which may explain why clubmakers seemed to have turned to ash at some point, since ash would make a stiffer shaft than hazel.

Ash shafts became the wood of choice for clubs until hickory came along around 1820 and demonstrated considerable lasting power because it had a steely spring to it and was deemed far superior to any other woods for making a shaft. The shaft revolutionized the game of golf.

Hickory quickly established itself as being superior to ash, because it has a great deal of strength, is light and absorbs shock. Originally in abundance in the southern regions of the United States, particularly the Tennessee

Assortment of antique clubs, balls, trophies, and scorecards guaranteed to draw the collector's eye.

hickory belt, the popularity of this shaft contributed greatly to an eventual shortage of the prized wood. Ringed hickory shafts cut from the center of the trunk were the most desired, since they were much tougher than hickory cut from other portions of the tree.

Clubmakers determined that the most effective shafts were made of a variety of red hickory, preferably cut from the center of the tree. Center cut hickory grain had a circular look to it, and shafts made from this part of the tree were noted to have "ring" hickory. The death of the hickory shaft resulted from an increasing demand in relation to a decreasing supply of hickory trees. Clubmakers were basically forced into finding a replacement for the well regarded hickory shaft.

The Bulger

When the gutta percha ball arrived toward the second part of the 19th century, the long nosed woods were found to be more easily damaged by the harder and heavier gutty. The result was that by 1880, wooden head clubs were designed to reflect the changes in the game because of golf's new ball. Clubheads were moving toward a shorter, broader shape, with a deeper face. In short, the "Bulger" was born.

The bulger's design was so scientifically sound that modern clubs are still produced in this mold. Credit for this design usually goes to Willie Park Junior and Henry Lamb. Park claimed he invented the club in 1883, but gives Lamb the credit for conceiving the name, "bulger." Whatever the origin, scientists concede that a ball struck with the type of convex surface such as the face of a bulger will produce less hook or slice than the concave surface of a long nose wood. The results on the course were even more convincing, and the long nose driver with the hooked face had seen its day.

That is not to say that clubmakers completely gave up on long nose woods. Some experimented with clubs that maintained the long, narrow aspect of the clubhead, but employed a convex face. But it was too late, of course, and the bulger shaped clubs became the club of choice for the golfing public.

The new bulger-shaped wooden heads permitted the clubmakers to improve the method by which shafts were now attached to the clubhead. The bulky, wider head on the bulger made it easier for clubmakers to drill a hole for a tapered shaft to be inserted into. Other techniques of the times were the mortise, the twin-splice and V-insert, but the bore-through socket design was so sound, that it is still used today, even on steel shafted woods. With the advent of the socket head wood came new methods to replace whipping. Some clubmakers replaced the twine with brass bands which, they claimed,

Array of bulgur clubs.

strengthened the neck of the club as well as improved it from a visual perspective.

Clubmakers also began experimenting with inserts on the bulgers, and everything from glass, rubber, elephant hide and ivory were used to protect the bulger's face from striking the hard gutta percha. Ultimately, strips of metal, coil springs, and even ball bearings were tested to improve distance and trajectory. While most of these inventions and experiments failed, some proved scientifically sound and are used in the design of clubs even today.

Once golfers committed to the bulger design, it wasn't long before the baffy came along to replace the baffing spoon. The baffy was a small headed, highly lofted wood which, despite the popularity of irons at the end of the 19th century, enjoyed a great deal of popularity because of the distance the club produced and the ease of which the club lofted the ball off the fairway.

The bulger design also paved the way for the brassie, a wood with more loft than a driver, but not quite as much as the baffy. The brassie was used off the tee quite successfully because its shorter shaft and higher loft made it easier to hit straight.

Golf clubs with aluminum heads began to appear in the game at the end of the 19th century as well. One of the most popular metalwoods designers was William Mills of England who developed a very successful putter,

and by 1892 began experimented with various aluminum clubheads. In his early metalwood clubheads, Mills would insert three wooden inserts so that the gutty ball would be met with wood on impact. But by 1900, Mills was the first clubmaker to make an aluminum wood that did not feature inserts made of wood or any other material for that matter. Mills manufactured the clubs and marketed them as unbreakable and economical, since they would not be damaged by water and did not demand constant cleaning. Yet the aluminum clubs, while popular, did not replace the more traditional woods, which flourished well into the 20th century.

THE IRONS

The earliest clubmakers, who were by trade carpenters and bowmakers, were already experts on the implementation of wood in their designs of golf clubs.

But when an iron clubhead was desired, it was the blacksmiths who picked up the ball, so to speak. However, the demand for irons was relatively minute in golf's early days. With the feathery ball, a wood club was still the desired club of choice, since an iron was more likely to do damage to the leather cased featheries.

Still, there were certain types of shots that the average Scottish course required. Chiefly, shots from the tall gorse, or sand bunkers or general hardpan surfaces

Assorted smooth-faced clubs pre-1900.

where a wooden club might likely be damaged. Therefore, it is believed that the earliest irons were made exclusively for hazard shots.

Blacksmiths, whose work mostly comprised of shoeing horses and making farm implements, were only too happy to pick up extra work they picked up from wealthy golfers in search of improving their game. Early irons were often large and heavy and players were discouraged from using them on the course because of the giant divots they often left in their wake. They were also expensive to make—twice the cost of a wood, so there weren't a lot of them around. In fact, an "early iron" is still considered by collectors to be any iron made prior to 1850.

To make an iron, a blacksmith would begin with a flat piece of iron a few inches wide and nearly a foot long. After heating it, he would flatten half of the strip so that it was twice as thick as when he began. The thin part was then wrapped around to form a hosel, then hammered again to create the desired loft and lie. The face was hammered to give it a concave face and left plain. Once the blacksmith did this, the head would be given to a clubmaker who shafted and gripped the club.

These early irons had names like "heavy iron," "bunker iron," and "spade." They were often crude in appearance, but they served their purpose, which was to advance the golf ball from hazardous places. Playing a ball from where it lies, in Scotland, often meant hitting through mud, cart tracks, driftwood and grass so thick that it may have occurred to golfers at some point to bring along a sword. The clubhead had to be quite heavy because the golfer needed mass behind his swing to clear the ball from the hazards. Collectors often note that early irons have significant denting because of the manner in which these clubs were used.

These heavy-headed irons also demanded strong shafts, like ash, as well as a very thick grip to execute the shots required of them. The early 17th and 18th century irons were held into place on the shaft by a joining method with serrated knopping at the top of the hosel. Later into the 19th century, rivets began to be used to firmly hold the shaft and the iron head together.

By 1850, iron niblicks and track irons, also known as general purpose irons, became more popular. The term "track" referred to the many cart tracks that appeared on links courses of the time, since farmers used to transport seaweed from the shore to their farms for fertilizing purposes. The wheels, with their wet loads, would sink down into the turf about two inches thick. The Scottish, with no affinity for winter rules or free drops, were faced with lies that would be difficult, if not downright unfair, to say the least. To play out of such lies, the blacksmith made a special iron with a small enough head to get behind the ball.

From left to right, a track iron pre-1890, a heavy soled niblick from 1900, a smooth faced sand iron from 1935, and Young's sand iron from 1929.

Such rut irons were either simply round, small headed irons, or sometimes a rut iron with a cut-off toe.

Rut irons or "rutters" came to be used in bunkers as well, but because of their small faces, they did not always produce the desired intent. With the feathery ball sitting in sand, an explosion shot was the shot of choice, since a skulled or topped shot with an iron was likely to render the feathery useless. Therefore, not too many irons were found in a player's bag. The damage to the expensive feather ball being the reason.

By the time the gutta percha ball arrived in 1848, golf became available to the masses because the expense of a golfball had dropped considerably. Most importantly, iron clubs did not destroy gutties, so more people began carrying more and more irons. This increased demand for irons enabled blacksmiths to set aside some of their other metal work and focus their efforts on the world of iron clubmaking. These new "cleekmakers" soon found themselves specializing in certain iron heads and many of them produced clubs for different clubmakers. The more renown they became, the more likely it was for them to begin stamping their names or marking the backs of the iron heads as a signature.

By the late 1800s, irons began to flatten out and the heavy track irons began to fall by the wayside. Cleekmakers were soon hiring dozens of men to meet the demands of golfers, and a cleekmaking company often had certain specialists. The bigger and stronger men were often "hammer men" who did all the heavy and more physical work. Others worked with dies for the stamping and grooving of patterns on the face of the club so that golfers could put spin on the ball.

One of the major problems a clubmaker faced when assembling an iron was to ensure that the shaft was tapered perfectly to fit the hosel of the club. If there was any give or action at the hosel, the club would be useless, so they took great pains to ensure that cleekmakers extended the hosel to the very heel of the club, enabling the clubmaker to drive the shaft down to the sole of the club. This ensured a very tight fit and made it possible for the cleekmaker to make an even shorter hosel, creating a lighter club, and balancing the clubhead so that there was more weight behind the ball on impact.

With the advent of these less clunky irons, golfers began using "cleeks" on parts of the course that were formerly taboo for irons. Now, cleeks were being used for approach shots to the green, as soft, lofted shots were possible with these irons. Golfers were finding out that lofted shots were more playable with these lighter irons than the old baffing spoon, and "mashies" and "niblicks" were born.

Serious collectors have learned the names of the clubmakers who stamped their names on the clubs they

Niblicks from 1935–1945.

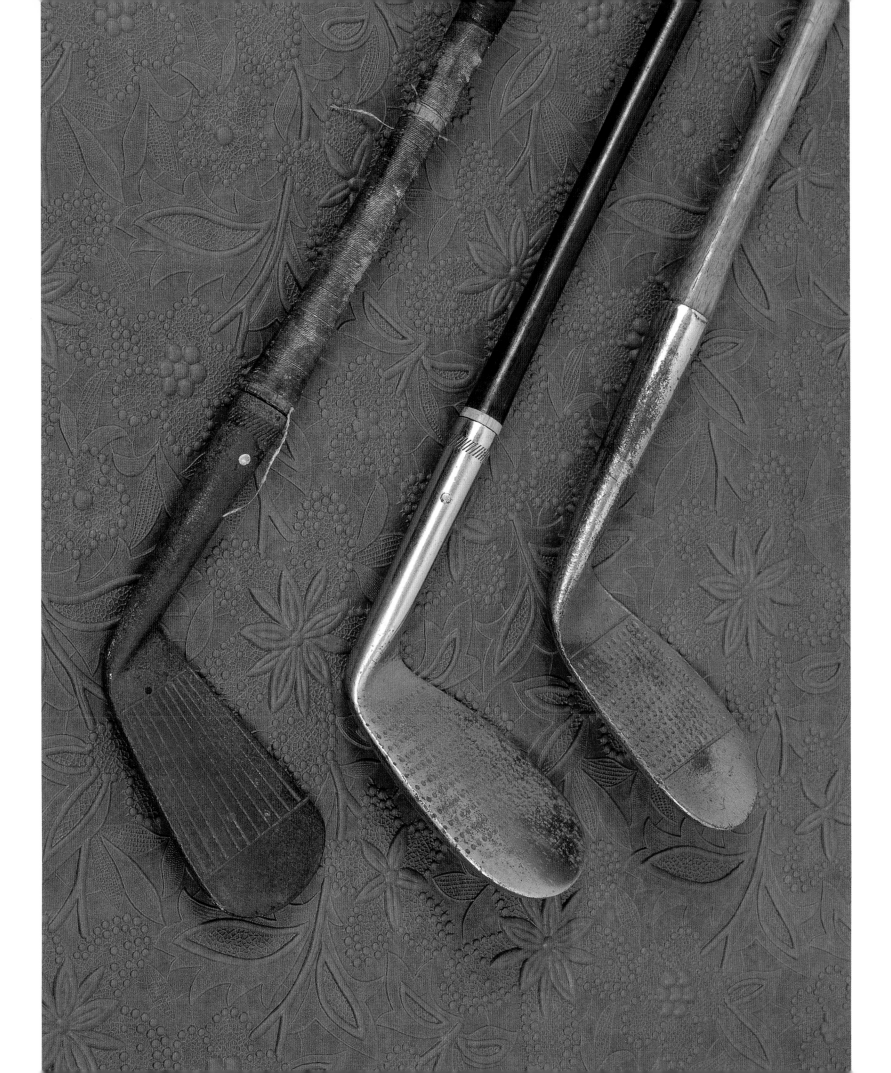

produced, since families and individual clubmakers often had certain specialties that golfers desired. Blacksmiths who worked alone generally did not put their named on the clubs they made, but there are some cleekmakers who were renown for their quality and collectors continue to seek out these clubs.

One noted cleekmaker from Musselburgh was the Carrick family, which formed F.& A. Carrick in 1840. Carrick's irons were the first known irons to carry trademarks, which were marked with a simple "X", sometimes with the Carrick name stamped on the head. The family continued to produce clubs of a very high quality right through the turn of the century.

The Anderson family at Anstruther in Fife had a very successful cleekmaking company which, by the end of the 19th century, was producing 40,000 iron clubheads a year. The company was probably best known for developing the patent on the Carruthers Cleek, an iron with a short hosel in which the shaft was brought right through the hosel down to the sole, forming one of the sturdiest irons to date. On early clubs, the Anderson family stamped their name, but later switched to a trademark "Arrow."

Old Tom Morris, working out of St. Andrews, stamped his name on many irons, and the name familiarity has always drawn collectors to his work. By 1880, golfers now had several irons in their bag, but the one club making the most noise seemed to be the mashie, and by the end of the century, the club was in wide circulation among golfers. Comparable to a 5 iron today, the mashie achieved a great deal of attention when J.H. Taylor began to hit it with great success in several Open victories. Taylor, known for his control of his iron shots, had a strong, short swing and seemed to stop his balls on the green with remarkable skill. When it was known that Taylor was playing a mashie, golfers went to the club in droves.

The success of the mashie led to driving mashies, deep-faced mashies and even the mashie-niblick. Eventually, the mashie spun off other clubs, such as "the glory iron," the "spade niblick," the "sky iron," the "jigger," and the "sammy." The result was that greenskeepers now had a new problem. Divots were tearing up their courses!

It wasn't until the 1920s when the idea of a clubmaker selling a matched set of irons took hold. Until then, a golfer might carry a small set of irons, or perhaps an assembly of mismatched irons made by different clubmakers, according to either his specialty or the golfer's desire. But in the mid 1920s, manufacturers such as A.G. Spalding began offering a matching set of irons rather than individually priced ones.

One of the most popular Scottish cleekmakers was Tom Stewart, who gained even more fame when the world's greatest golfer, Bobby Jones, used irons Stewart

Mid-irons from the early 1900s.

had made for him. Stewart then sought to cash in on Jones' success by offering "R.T.J. Model" clubs until Jones, also an attorney, asked him to cease. It wasn't until after Jones, who kept his amateur status throughout his playing career, retired in 1930, that he entered into an agreement to allow Spalding to market his golf clubs under the Jones signature. Once matching sets became the norm, the modern era of irons was born.

Ironically, steel shafts had been experimented with in the late 19th century, but the top clubmakers couldn't seem to make them work. They were simply too heavy to replace hickory shafts. However, the golf world was beginning to exhaust the supply of quality hickory for shafts, and golf manufacturers were worried. They referred to their problem as the "hickory famine," and began lobbying both the USGA and the R & A to consider making them legal. Curiously, there were no rules specifically against using steel shafts, and by the time manufacturers had begun to make hollow, tapered steel shaft which were not quite as heavy as their predecessors, both governing golf associations became worried and barred their use.

But by 1925, the USGA had fully recognized the problem, and in 1929, the R & A followed suit. Steel shafted clubs had become highly desired and there was no turning back. The hickory shafted clubs were now collector's items.

THE PUTTERS
Long nose putters

The putters used in the long nose era were usually quite versatile clubs, especially on Scottish links courses. Beyond putting, these clubs were often called upon for long bump and run shots from off the green, as well as lag putts over undulating grounds just off the green. To understand putters as equipment it is important to understand what role putting played in the early days of golf. The old links courses were very difficult to play around the hole. In fact, one of the earliest rules of golf states that a player, upon holing out, must tee up his ball within one club's length of the hole just played. One can only imagine what the area around the hole must have been like.

However, in the early days of golf, putting was not as important as it is today. It was possible to post a fine score by doing particularly well in the long game, and putting was often considered more a matter of luck. Golfers might complain about the unfairness of a missed putt, but it was probably with good reason. They often had to contend with "cupped lies" on the green.

The old wooden long nose putters looked quite similar to drivers of the times, and even had the same type of hooked face. However, putters were heavier, with shorter shafts and maintained a more vertical lie. Because the summer months in Scotland often produced

An assortment of early putters from left to right, a Schenectady putter, a wooden head win skeet brass face, a smooth face putter, a rye neck putter, and a Mills of Sunderland aluminum case putter.

dry, unwatered and hard, dusty fairways, stopping the ball on the green to set up a putt was a tricky matter. Fortunately, the architects of golf had designed courses which had the hazards off to the sides of the greens, allowing players to use bump and run shots to the green.

These types of required shots on links courses led to the development of specialty putters, such as the driving putter. The driving putter was designed for the purpose of making long bump putts, and for hitting the ball low against a heavy wind. This club was basically a long, stiff shaft attached to a putter head. Not as popular as spoons and regular putters, these clubs were often used to skim the ball across the terrain. Scotswomen of the day might play an entire round with a driving putter, since the ground was often so dry, a ball could be advanced 100 yards easily with a driving putter.

Because of the way the game was played in Scotland on the links courses, it was necessary to have several putters to use for different shots. Putters for short putts and holing out were entirely different than the putters used to, say, advance the ball onto the green. The approach putter was another club that saw heavy use in the early days of golf. Similar to the driving putter, the approach putter was often used after a drive, depending

Golfers might complain about the unfairness of a missed putt, but it was probably with good reason.

on the length of the hole, to play a running shot to a desired area of the green. Depending upon how the ball was struck, the putt might bounce along the ground, or behave like a chip shot before settling down to a roll.

Upon the arrival of the gutta percha ball, the game experienced a dramatic increase in iron play because irons were not as hazardous to the life of a gutty ball as opposed to a feathery. Since it was easier with an iron to loft a ball onto a green and impart spin to control the way it landed, it was generally thought that it might also be a good idea to use an iron for putting as well.

The first iron blade putters had a little loft to them and putting cleeks became quite popular. By 1885, the wooden putter pretty much disappeared from the scene, and when Willie Park Junior patented the "Bent neck putter" (also referred to as a "wry-necked putter") around this time, a new design in putting technology was reached, and many of Park's original designs are still used today.

The bent neck putter had a bend in the hosel (similar to an offset) which had the effect of putting the ball in direct line with the shaft. Once this design was in place, clubmakers began to experiment a great deal with putters, and because of the increased importance that putting now has in golf, putter designs are, to this day, con-

Faces of mid-irons.

stantly reworked and redesigned in an attempt to improve a golfer's scores.

In 1895, William Mills of Sunderland, England who would eventually become the most prolific designer of aluminum headed golf clubs, produced an aluminum clubhead frame which was filled with wood. Five years later, he would produce a clubhead made entirely of aluminum, and a golfer by the name of James Braid, who had never demonstrated much prowess as a putter, began winning Open Championships using a Mills aluminum putter. That same year, Harold Hilton used a Mills putter to capture the British Amateur, and aluminum putters became enormously popular.

Around the turn of the century, golfers had a wide variety of putters to choose from, provided they had the patience to experiment. Drilled face putters with holes punched through a deep, offset blade, apparently to reduce the distance a putt will travel, became just one of many unusual looking clubs designed for putting. Tom Morris produced a cylinder head putter, also called a drain pipe putter, in the early 1890s and it led to a series of cylinder designs and convex blades which followed.

In 1900, Willie Dunn Jr., winner of the open American championship received a patent on August 14th that covered a putter which was designed especially for the Haskell ball. The putter featured a negative loft convex faced put-

ter, enabling it to strike the ball above its center and give it forward spin, similar to the way a ball is struck in billiards. The result was Dunn's Rotary mallet head putter, which achieved some popularity at the turn of the century.

However, in 1902, a man by the name of Arthur F. "Bill" Knight of a small city in upstate New York called Schenectady, set out to improve his own putting game by designing a putter he thought would answer his putting woes. He got the idea to try a putter with a flat head, but with the shaft inserted in the center, and with his engineering bent, decided to tackle the invention himself.

Knight tried a few versions with lead, hoping to achieve the kind of balance he felt was needed to give the club proper feel and weight distribution. The lead putter apparently did not work out too well, and Knight quickly relegated his prototype to the scrap heap. But when he attempted to fill the same mold with aluminum this time, he stumbled onto the putter that would eventually become the most renown putter the game of golf has ever known.

Scientifically, Knight believed that by placing the shaft in the center of the head, a golfer would produce less torque on impact, resulting in more consistency. He also felt that the shape of the Schenectady improved alignment and sight lines to the ball. While playing at his country club in Schenectady, Knight met with Devereux

Two mid-irons from the late 1890s.

Emmet, who happened to be a friend of the great Australian-born amateur golfer, Walter Travis. Emmet tried Knight's Schenectady putter, liked it, and showed it to Travis a few days later. It wasn't long afterwards when Knight received a telegram from Travis himself, ordering a putter just like Emmet's. Knight made two putters for Travis, one with slightly more loft, and Travis quickly proclaimed it the best putter he'd ever used.

Travis used the putter in the 1902 U.S. Open and finished second, prompting hundreds of orders for Knight's Schenectady putter. Knight recognized the demand for the putter and wanted to give it the name "Travis" putter, but Travis, perhaps out of modesty, declined, stating that he felt "Schenectady" would be a better name for the putter.

Knight applied for and was granted a patent for his putter, and the date of the patent, "March 24, 1903" was marked on most of the Schenectady putters. The next year, Walter Travis became the first person outside of the United Kingdom to win the British Amateur. He beat Edward "Ted" Blackwell in a showdown between golfers who demonstrated different skills. Blackwell was a long hitting power golfer and Travis simply outputted him in the end, adding a great deal of mystique to the Schenectady putter.

Today, the Schenectady putter is still a prized collector's item even though they are available in relative abundance.

Upon news of Travis' victory in Britain, demand for the Schenectady putter went through the roof. Spalding was now manufacturing the putters, and cleekmakers in St. Andrews were also flooded with demands for the new club. Unfortunately, there was a great deal of resentment toward Travis' victory, as many influential British golfers felt the putter gave Travis an unfair advantage. In 1910, the R & A finally ruled on the fate of the Schenectady putter, making it an illegal club. Thousands of clubheads in production in Scotland had to be dumped, and many felt the ruling body overreacted when banning the putter. The controversy was further flamed when, in 1911, the USGA ruled the Schenectady a legal putter, and many felt the strain between the two governing bodies of golf would not be good for the game. But as it turned out, the two bodies were able to work together, despite their differences. Finally, in 1951, the R & A lifted their ban against the Schenectady putter, as well as the other many center-shafted putters that had come into prominence. Ironically, Walter Travis, after igniting the world on fire with his putting prowess using the Schenectady, was never able to recapture the magic with the infamous putter again. Today, the Schenectady

Early 1900s clubs from the collection at Winged Foot Golf Club in Mamaroneck, New York.

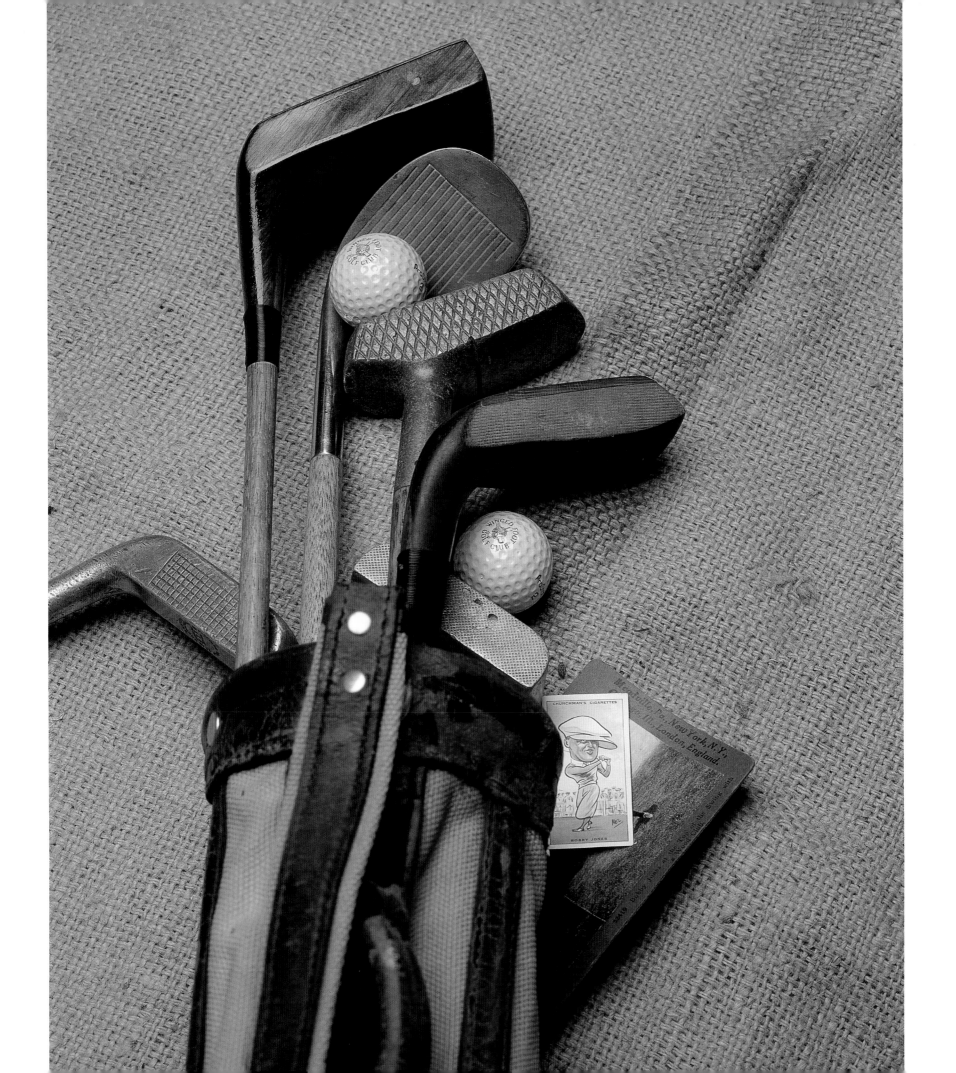

putter is still a prized collector's item even though they are available in relative abundance—a true reflection of their popularity at the time

Patent Clubs

There were several factors which led to the proliferation of patent clubs around the beginning of the 20th century. Perhaps the most significant was that interest in golf was reaching new heights. Golf courses were being built around the world quite rapidly to meet the growing legions of aspiring golfers in need of a place to play. Meanwhile, the industrial revolution enabled manufacturers to use new techniques which were not possible in earlier times. Hand forging was beginning to be replaced by mass production, and manufacturers looked for ways to cash in on the golf craze by pouring money into research and development of new clubs. All these factors contributed to the production of some of the oddest clubs imaginable, and collectors have this era to be quite thankful for.

While collectors of long nose woods and early irons are mostly drawn to a club's age and condition, the collector of patent clubs is generally inspired by a designer's creativity. Many collectors believe that patent clubs act as something of a bridge between the ancient and the modern clubs. If nothing else, they reflect the spirit of a golfer's neverending quest to improve his game. They also serve as a reminder of how the game has developed and how and why certain rules came into effect as well.

A patent is a legal document which is granted to an inventor, allowing him to produce and develop his idea for several years without competition. While nearly every golfclub ever made was patented, the term "patent club" to collectors, means any unusual club that may or may not have even been patented.

Patent clubs are generally very different in either their appearance or their construction from other collectible golf clubs. In many instances, patent clubs were prototype clubs which never made it to production. But they were well made and the intent to have them produced was genuine. The first patent golf club was granted in 1876 to Thomas Johnston, who intended to make long nose clubs from an Indian rubber called "vulcanite" or "ebonite." Not many of these clubs have ever been seen, and apparently, most of them were putters. From then on, inventors put a great deal of emphasis on patenting their designs, and it was not uncommon for clubmakers to mark clubs with either the patent date or "patent applied for" on the heads.

Among the most interesting patent clubs that turned up in the midst of patent club craze were the clubs which featured intriguing face treatments. The "Water" irons are

Assorted sand irons from 1880 to 1935.

among the most unusual. Water irons were designed at a time when many gutta percha balls on the market actually floated in water. Subsequently, it was not uncommon for a golfer to find his ball sitting atop a puddle of standing water, either on the fairway or in a bunker. The early golfer would therefore have to play the ball as it lied or suffer penalty strokes. One such water club was the "President" which was designed by W.G. Roy and featured a gaping hole right through the middle of the iron's clubface.

Also known as the ring mashie, the President performed well enough for Tom Morris to try his hand at the design of the club. But ultimately, it had inefficient balance and weight, and most troubling, four potential hitting surfaces to create further havoc. It wasn't surprising that the club eventually disappeared.

But other clubs with similar claims were quick to follow. "Rake" irons, which had slots and perforations that resembled a wide-toothed comb or rake came along, promising golfers an advantage in the sand, deep grass or water. Theoretically, the club, when swung, would allow obstructions such as water, sand and grass to pass through the clubface, while striking the ball unimpeded toward the target. Still, despite the apparent backing of some of the best golfers in the world at the time, rake irons did not gain much popularity. The prongs or teeth could easily become ensnared in the grass or ground and cause the clubhead to veer off line. Still, despite their uselessness on the course, downward pronged rake irons maintain high collector value because of their scarcity. Brown rake irons are particularly desirable because the teeth and perforations were surrounded with decorative engravings.

Despite the lack of popularity of Brown's rake irons, other noted cleek makers responded at the time with rake and water irons of their own. John S. Pearson produced mashies and niblicks with open slots in the back running horizontally across the clubface. His clubs also had another purpose beyond rescuing a ball from a lethal hazard. Pearson's irons were designed to create maximum backspin. But it seems that not many were actually made, since the clubs became illegal shortly after their introduction, and apparently, they were prone to break if swung at full force.

Also interesting from a visual perspective were the William F. Reach "waterfall" irons. These irons were designed to impart backspin on the ball, and the designs on the faces resembled waves of deep grooves. They were just one of many backspin irons to come along. Among them, ribbed and gridded irons, deep-dimple irons, and vertical-grooved irons, all of which were ultimately banned by both the R & A and the USGA. By 1924, slotted, ribbed, waffle faced or punched clubs with lines more than a given width were barred from competition, and the clubs ultimately disappeared. Apparently, these backspin clubs were well loved by the game's top golfers of the time because at the 1924 Southern California championship, bags were examined on the first tee and over 200 clubs had to be removed! Such was infiltration of backspin irons at the time.

Other designs, such as the anti-shank clubs, lifted the hosel connection to the top of the club and hoped to appeal to golfers with a case of the dreaded shanks. And flanged niblicks were designed to help players explode a ball out of a soft sand hazard.

Perhaps best known and desired by collectors are the adjustable or mechanical clubs which came into prominence at the end of the 19th century. The best known and most famous adjustable club is the Urquhart. A member of the Honourable Company of Edinburgh Golfers, Robert L. Urquhart came up with several patents for clubs which could be adjusted to many different lofts, both right and left handed, by simply pressing a button on the rear of the hosel and simultaneously pulling out and twisting the head of the club.

This was accomplished by a spring which was inserted into the iron socket at the end of the wooden shaft. The socket was something of a cog-wheel arrangement which prohibited the head from moving or even becoming loose. Ideally, a player would need only to carry one iron with him during a round.

Countless adjustable irons followed, with various means of adjusting the loft on the clubs, such as "all-in-one" clubs as they were called, or "emergency" clubs. Even metal shaft adjustable woods never amounted to much on the golf course and the were ultimately banned from competition. But that doesn't stop the average collector from delighting in these rare finds. Face inserts were used by some clubmakers to protect the area of impact on the ball, and some of the materials they used resulted in patent woods that are every bit as interesting as the irons of the patent era.

Brass, ivory and steel were some of the more common inserts on woods at the time. Then clubmakers began to experiment with the actual clubheads, with the most common being aluminum. Some clubmakers used molded and compressed synthetics in their efforts to come up with heads that could withstand the elements. But the most interesting patent woods clearly revolved around the shapes of the clubs themselves. At the turn of the century, most woods were descendants of the bulger design and all of them looked fairly similar. That is, until MacGregor unleashed the "Streamliner." The Streamliner looked like a bullet going backwards, and it was MacGregor's attempt at increasing clubhead speed through experimentation with aerodynamic properties. As a bonus to collectors, the Streamliner featured one of the earliest chromed steel shafts. Other patent woods featured unique designs to the neck, such as the Scott patent fork splice and the Spalding triple splice, which were designed to increase strength between the head and shaft.

If ever a club was designed and redesigned throughout golf history, the putter was it. No stroke in golf is quite so temperamental and streaky as the putt, and golfers are renown for their willingness to try something new on the putting green. One popular patent putter design revolved around the hosel and neck of the club.

Designers did everything they could to move the hosel back and away from the blade striking area, and bending the hosel back was the preferred method. Weighting the putter head for balance and feel was another popular form of patents on putters. Aside from the infamous "Schenectady" putter and other center shafted or forked hosel designs, the most interesting patent putters were the many adjustable putters that, like adjustable irons, could be changed to alter lie or loft on approach putts, or even left or right handed putts.

All in all, the early part of the 20th century produced a gold mine of patent clubs that are every bit as enjoyable for collectors as the era of long nose woods and early irons.

Assorted irons from 1870–1910.

GOLF
ACCESSORIES
AND
COLLECTIBLES

Credential buttons from golf tournaments worldwide.

Clubs and balls are the only thing a golfer needs to play a round, but collectors are well aware that rarely can a collection end there. The game of golf has produced too many interesting accessories, artifacts and odds and ends for the collector to turn his back on. The more familiar one becomes with the history of the game, the more golf memorabilia and collectibles will gain in appeal. And like the appeal of the patent clubs, the more interesting the design or invention, the better!

TEES

The golf tees used today are basically all the same. Cheap, disposable wooden tees which barely get a player's attention should he, after a drive, notice that his tee has split into two pieces. However, 500 years ago, golfers were looking to elevate the ball on the turf, and an evolution in the design of golf tees followed. The earliest tees were most likely tees created by a golfer's heel imprint in the ground. This method raised the ground behind the heel and a player was able to create a desired lie from which to hit the ball. In fact, there are still tour players who do this from time to time off the tee, especially on par three holes where an iron would be the club of choice.

The next stage in golf tee design centered around the formation of small mounds of dirt or sand which a ball could be rested upon to create elevation. Golfers (or caddies) would do this by hand until the invention of the sand tee mold captured the imagination of the golf world shortly before the turn of the 20th century. Since making a tee by hand was a very time consuming and dirty practice, the sand tee mold enabled golfers to begin forming consistent tees without the mess.

Since golf tees are relatively inexpensive, they're a great way to start a golf collection. There are literally hundreds of different tee brands from the 1930s alone.

Made of various shapes and sizes, sand tee molds were often made of aluminum or stainless steel, and usually featured some type of spring plunger. A golfer would scoop up some moist sand or dirt, pack it into the mold, then depress the "button" or plunger to form a consistent sand or dirt tee. Sand tee molds were considered a great improvement over existing tee making by hand, but the golf invention craze that occurred in the early 1900s with clubs and ball patterns also affected the design of the golf tee.

Self-adjusting golf tees which resembled giant tweezers, cupped-dome tees made of plastic, rubber tees with round weights on one end, and brass tees with rubber arms that swiveled after impact were all inventions that made their way into golf by the 1930s. Tees were also being made of every material imaginable, such as aluminum, steel, paper, wire, rubber and zinc, to name a few. In fact, greenskeepers had the most to say about the abolition of wire tees, which would often entangle their mower blades.

The shape of tees was also a great experimental ground for inventors, as triangles, stars, tethers and spinners all saw their day in the sun. Ultimately, however, the plain wooden peg emerged as the cheapest, simplest and least cumbersome method of elevating a golf ball. When this was realized, manufacturers turned to packaging to set their tees apart from the rest. The pack-

aging and marketing of tees beginning in the 1920s is something that the sport no longer enjoys.

Walter Hagen endorsed "The Yello Tee," a simple wooden peg, which he famously left in the ground after every tee shot. Once the last player in his group left the tee box, a scene not unlike the aftermath of a foul ball hit into the stands at a baseball game would follow, with fans and collectors scrambling for Hagen's tee!

Packaging concepts for tees included cloth bags, boxes of all sizes and matchbook-like packets with ornate designs and often outlandish claims, guaranteeing lower scores. To many, a tee is just a tee in today's game, and manufacturers wouldn't waste a penny trying any marketing strategy beyond keeping the cost low. In the roaring '20s, the golf tee was an accessory that collectors today are quite thankful for.

GOLF BAGS AND CARRIERS

Awkward as it might have been, for centuries, golfers and their caddies carried golf clubs under their arms without the benefit of any devices or contraptions. One of the reasons it wasn't necessary to carry some kind of bag or carrier is because players rarely played a round with more than seven clubs. And if they did, it was generally the caddie who bore the brunt of the extra load.

In the late 1800s, bags or covers came into usage so

A caddie bag from the 1870s.

that golfers could keep the grips from getting wet in the traditionally damp Scottish weather. The earliest bags were made of cloth but had no handles or straps. Only sacks, really, with the sole purpose to keep clubs dry rather than make carrying them any easier. Usually made of brown sack cloth or canvas, these simple sacks are the rarest of golf bags. Eventually, bag designers turned to leather to cover the base of golf bags so that the cloth would not become soaked when rested on wet grounds. Circular rings were then added to make the insertion and removal of clubs easier. Before long, handles and shoulder straps were added, as well as three and four stays, which kept the bags stiff and prevented them from folding or collapsing. Ball pockets as well as pockets large enough to carry golf clothing were added along the way, as leather became the material of choice for golf bag design.

Called "caddy bags" at the turn of the century, they began to have the manufacturer's name lettered on the side, as well as the golfer's name in many cases. The bags were getting larger and larger and heavier as well, due to the increased usage of leather on the entire bag. Earlier bags had circular openings with smaller diameters such as three or four inches, but as the size of the

In the roaring '20s, the golf tee was an accessory that collectors today are quite thankful for.

bags increased, so did the number of clubs golfers wanted to carry!

Smaller "quiver" bags, called such because they resembled the holders that archers would use for their arrows, were now giving way to large leather bags, up to eight inches in diameter and made of different grades of hide, such as elk, kid leather and suede.

Unfortunately for collectors, leather, unless oiled and treated on a regular basis, has a tendency to deteriorate after half a century or so. Broken straps and handles are the most common problem, followed by deterioration or rotting of the leather itself. Wicker bags and other patent bags are considered rare finds among collectors.

The other less common devices were the club carriers, which featured dozens of different designs, ranging from stands, satchels and rings. Bipod legs, common on bags today, were actually in use in the late 1800s as golfers sought ways to play the game without the help of caddies. The most renown carrier equipment is referred to as "Osmond's Patent" and commands the highest value among collectors. But other makers, such as George Bussey of London, were well known at the time for high quality carriers which collectors still seek today.

Golf-themed whiskey bottles from the 1920s.

OTHER COLLECTIBLES

There are countless golf collectibles from decanters and cocktail sets to ashtrays and match safes, all with golf themes and valued at whatever someone is willing to pay for them. Visual appeal or historical significance are often what makes these collectibles desirable. Golf scene ceramics, pins, badges, and figurines are just a few of many different areas of golf memorabilia that exist, and the amount of variety is limited only to the maker's imagination.

Some collectors are drawn to the numerous trophies and medals in existence, all of varying quality and significance, and, of course, price. Still, if a collector wants a British Open medal won by Bobby Locke, and has upwards of $50,000 to spend, he might very well be able to add such a medal to his collection. On more modest terms, collectors are often drawn to smaller medals demanding considerably less on the open market, but each with a story behind it.

The same goes for trophies, goblets and cups. Often, the esthetic value is more important to collectors, since hand-craftsmanship at the beginning of the 20th century, when these golf artifacts flourished, was the rule of the day. Bronze golfers atop elaborate marble bases and sterling silver loving cups, often with a golfing scene depicted, are popular golf objects for collectors because of the ease of which they can be displayed. They just look nice on a mantle or bookshelf!

Golf art is another category of collectibles which many collectors delight in because the nature of collecting golf art often entails research and study. In the 17th century in Holland, Dutch painters were drawn to winter scenes, and it was not uncommon for them to depict golf being played on frozen ponds. Drawings by Avercamp, which are displayed in the Royal Collection at Dresden and believed to be done in the year 1610, show golfers in remarkably modern poses such as lining up putts, where, were it not for the fashions depicted, it would be difficult to date them. Unfortunately, the Scots did not have any versions of "Dutch Masters" to paint the game of golf as they saw it in Scotland at the time. But toward the end of the 18th century, portraits of golfers with caddies and clubs begin to appear. These paintings have been translated to elaborate mezzotints which were famous in their day, and their depictions of various baffies and spoons were of great value to historians.

Some early depictions of Scottish golf, such as John Smart's *St. Andrew's Hell Bunker* and Garden G. Smith's *The Black Shed at Hoylake* are considered tremendously valuable watercolor paintings from the late 1800s, not to mention beautiful from a visual perspective as well.

Many collectors enjoy collecting rare, out-of-print golf books.

GOLF BOOKS

Golf books don't always command the kind of respect and value that other collectibles such as gutty balls and long nose woods do, but that's not an indication of the amount of pleasure a rare golf book can provide. After all, you can only look at a gutty for so long, but a book can be perused and studied for hours and days on end.

W.W. Tulloch's, *The Life of Tom Morris* is a rare and valuable book written as an 87th birthday present to Old Tom by a fellow member of the Royal and Ancient Club of St. Andrews in 1908. Tulloch painstakenly recounts the rich and bittersweet life of the legendary Scot, and the book is packed with poetic tributes to the man who captured the spirit of golf like no other.

Another charming and collectible book is Francis Ouimet's *A Game of Golf*, where Ouimet, the miraculous young winner of the 1913 U.S. Open at Brookline, documents his life, including his dramatic and unlikely victory against the likes of Harry Vardon and Ted Ray. If for no other reason than the cover art, these rare books make great collectibles because, once found, they can continue to be used and enjoyed by the collector. You wouldn't think about throwing a long nose wood in your bag and testing it on the range, but the golf book collector is almost sure to read the books he collects!

ODDS AND ENDS

With baseball card collections demanding record prices, it's no surprise that golf cards have taken a ride on baseball's coattails. Beginning in around 1880, tobacco companies needed some kind of stiff cardboard to prevent a pack of cigarettes from being bent or crushed. Since men made up the majority of smokers, companies often featured military and sports-themed cards in their packaging. Tobacco's success with these cards quickly spread into the packaging of magazines, cereals and chewing gum, and lo and behold, an industry of collecting was born. The American Tobacco Series of Champion Athletes and prize fighters of 1910 released the Mecca cigarette set, which included six American golfers who were among the top players at the time. The British also released a series of golf cards in their Guinea Gold cigarette packs, including Old Tom Morris and Harry Vardon.

While most single golf cards don't command values comparable to that of a Babe Ruth rookie card in baseball, there are several complete golf sets of cards, such as the Burline sets from 1910 in England, which are valued at over $20,000 in mint condition. Still, you might want to hold onto that Tiger Woods card!

Cigarette cards from 1910 to 1935.

COLLECTOR'S GLOSSARY

"In the Rough" cocktail, a popular post-round drink for golfers in the 1920s.

Baffing spoon or baffy spoon: A wooden club which was the shortest, stiffest and most lofted club in a set of spoons. A golfer would use this club primarily for an approach shot. The modern equivalent is a wedge.

Baffy: A small headed, steeply lofted wooden club developed from the baffing spoon.

Balata: A hard, resilient substance derived from the gum of a bully or balata tree in either South America or the West Indies. Balata has been used in the making of rubber-cored golf balls, and is still popular among better golfers today who prefer "feel" balls rather than the more durable surlyn-covered balls.

Bap-headed: In the late 19th and early 20th century, these wooden clubs were more rounded in shape as opposed to the long nose woods made earlier.

Blade putter: A putter with the blade and neck of the same form of a golfer's standard irons.

Boxwood: The earliest known and rarest golf balls, these balls were often made of beech or boxroot.

Bramble: The small molded bumps on the surface of late gutta percha balls as well as early rubber-core balls, intended to improve the aerodynamic properties (similar to dimples) of a golf ball.

Brassie or brassy: Various lofted woods in the late 1880s were fitted with a brass sole plate. It is also a term for a wooden club which is lofted more than the driver but less than the spoon, and made with a brass sole plate. Later, a brassie became a term for a two wood.

Bulger: A wooden club, usually a driver with a slightly convexed face rather than just a flat surface.

Calamity Jane: A putter modeled on the Calamity Jane hickory-shafted blade putter made famous by Bobby Jones.

Chipper: A club used for chip shots, which often resembles an ancient mashie, i.e. a short shafted club.

Cleek: Derived from the Scotch word "click" meaning "hook," a cleek can be any of the numerous narrow-bladed irons, which can be used for long shots as well as approach shots or even hazard shots. The main characteristic of a cleek is that they are narrow-bladed and generally light. The cleek can also be a term for the one iron, as well as the four wood. Generally, the word is used today to describe a lofted wood with a shallow face.

Clubhead: The part of the club where the ball is struck. Usually made of wood or iron before the 20th century. The clubface is the actual surface on the clubhead which strikes the ball.

Golf tees used from 1900–1920.

Compression: The degree of resilience of a golf ball. A ball's compression is generally a measure of its hardness. The harder the ball, the less it will compress. The average compression of today's balls are 90 and 100.

Deep-faced: A club which is relatively thick when measured from top to bottom. Today's oversized drivers are deep-faced.

Dimple: The roundish depression on the surface of the golf ball.

Driver: The club that is one of the two longest hitting woods in a player's bag. Usually the number one wood, the modern drivers have an average loft between 8.5 and 12 degrees and a length over 43 inches.

Driving iron: A low lofted long iron, usually the 1 iron, this club is usually the most difficult club to hit well.

Driving mashie: An iron club with less loft than that of the mashie-iron, used for driving and for long shots to the green.

Driving putter: A straight faced wooden club used for driving low shots against the wind, this club was used in the early 19th century as a bump and run-type club.

Face or clubface: The striking surface of a clubhead.

Fairway wood: A wooden club that was used typically on the fairway or light rough and generally not the driver.

Featherie or feathery: A feather-stuffed, leather-covered ball used prior to the gutta percha ball in 1848. A feathery was usually stuffed with wet cow hair or feathers, and stuffed into a leather casing, also wet. When the feathers or hair dried, they would expand, and when the leather casing dried, it would shrink. The result was a very hard, round golf ball that lasted for centuries, until ultimately replaced by the cheaper, more durable gutty ball.

Flange: A projecting part on the back of an iron, the flange helps prevent the club from digging too deeply into the grass or sand. Thinner flanged clubs have less bounce and enable a golfer to cut down and under a ball, while sandwedges have a larger flange, adding bounce to the club. Putters may also be flanged.

Flip wedge: A highly lofted wedge, much like today's lob wedge.

Goose-neck: The neck of a club that is curved so much that the heel becomes slightly offset from the line of the shaft.

Grass club: A driver with slightly more loft than a straight-faced driver or play club. Usually with a stiffer handle and heavier head, a "grassed" club generally meant the club was "lofted."

An assortment of grass clubs from the mid-1900s.

Grip: The part of the shaft of a golf club which the player holds. In early golf, the grip was usually made with leather or pigskin, and later, rubber or some other synthetic material. The grip is also a term for the manner in which a golf club is held by a golfer.

Groove: This term refers to the linear scoring on a clubface. Clubmakers have long experimented with different types of grooves on clubfaces, similar to the way ballmakers have experimented with dimples on a golf ball.

Gutta or Gutta Percha: From the Malayan getah-percha sap tree, gutta percha was a resilient, easily molded substance from which golf balls were made beginning in 1848 until the early part of the 20th century. Some clubmakers also experimented with gutta percha to make clubheads, but the practice was quickly abandoned. The gutta percha was less expensive to make than its predecessor, the feathery, and therefore opened golf up to a broader section of the population.

Gutty or guttie: A gutta percha ball.

Gutty-perky: The Scottish variant of the gutta percha ball.

Head: See clubhead.

Heel: The near end of a clubhead directly below the neck.

Hickory: The wood from a North American tree from the Carya genus, hickory was used beginning in the early 19th century to the 1920s for making the shafts of golf clubs because of its toughness.

Hosel: This is the neck or socket in an iron clubhead.

Iron: A golf club with the head made of iron, or in modern times, an iron may be made of steel or titanium. An iron made prior to 1850 was likely to be heavily lofted and used mainly for playing out of trouble. Players had heavy irons and light irons and possibly even an iron putter, and all may have been referred to as irons. By 1890, irons were being classified as cleeks, mashies, niblicks and putters, according to the desired shot.

Jigger: A moderately lofted, shallow-faced and short-shafted iron that was designed for approach shots in the early 20th century, specifically chip shots.

Lie: The angle in which a clubhead is set on a shaft. This angle is measured between the shaft and the horizontal, when the club is properly soled by a golfer at address.

Links: Generally referred to as low-lying seaside land on the east coast of the Scottish Lowlands. Because of the short bent grass and natural windswept dunes and undulating turf, the land was the perfect setting for the earliest golfers. Today, links courses have been constructed all over the world to simulate the terrain of the earliest Scottish golf courses.

An assortment of early grips.

Loft: The degree to which a clubface is tipped back from vertical. This angle is measured as the angle between the face and a line parallel to the shaft.

Lofted: A club that has a relatively steep loft on the face.

Lofting Iron: A club used in the late 19th century for approach shots, ultimately replaced by the pitching mashie.

Long Irons: Generally considered to be the 1, 2, and 3 numbered irons, these clubs are typically used for long approach shots from the fairway, or for shots off the tee where it was desired to keep the ball low and below the wind.

Mallet or Mallethead: A putter which has a head that is significantly wider and heavier than that of a blade putter.

Mashie: A lofted iron club that was introduced around 1880 and used for imparting spin on a pitch shot. The club quickly became the most popular approach club in a golfer's bag. The mashie later became a term for the 5 iron.

Mashie-iron: An iron club which was less lofted than a mashie and used mainly for full shots to the green or off the tee. The mashie-iron also became a name for the 4 iron.

Mashie-niblick: An iron club that had a loft between that of a mashie and a niblick. Used for pitching, a mashie-niblick could also refer to a 6 or 7 iron.

Matched Clubs: Clubs that were designed and made in a graded and numbered series with consistent specifications, characteristics and swingweights.

Middle Spoon or Mid-spoon: A wooden club used in the late 19th century, and having a loft between those of a long spoon and a short spoon.

Mid-iron: An iron club which had more loft than a driving iron. It was also an alternate name for the 2 iron.

Mid-mashie: An alternate name for the 3 iron.

Neck: The tapered projecting section of a wooden clubhead where the shaft is fitted.

Niblick: Of the Scottish word meaning "short-nose" the niblick was a short-headed, highly lofted wood, used for trouble shots and tight lies and much shorter in the nose than any other wooden club. An iron niblick was a deep-bladed club that was more steeply lofted than a mashie and used mostly for playing from the sand and rough. The niblick is also an alternate name for the 9 iron.

Nose: The toe of a wooden club.

Offset: A crooked neck or hosel which sets the clubhead slightly off the line of the shaft. This is done on some putters to improve sight lines to the ball. It is also done on irons and woods to help golfers square the clubface at impact.

Assorted irons, including from top to bottom, a scored face iron from the early 1900s, a back stop mashie from 1917, a dot iron faced club from the early 1900s, and a smooth faced iron from 1905.

Peg: A tee.

Pimple: See bramble.

Pitching irons: The short irons.

Pitching wedge: An iron club used mainly for playing pitch shots to the green. These clubs are highly lofted and have less bounce than that of a sand wedge.

Play club: The earlier name for the straightest-faced, longest hitting wood which was later called the driver.

President: This was an iron club that had a steep loft similar to that of a niblick, with a hole through the face. It was a club that was used for playing out of the water.

Putter: A golf club designed for putting on or near the green. A putter usually has a very upright lie as well as a short shaft. Up until the 1850s, putters were made of wood until iron became the preferred putter clubhead.

Putty: The Eclipse ball, which was softer than the gutta percha.

Rake: A lofted iron club which had vertical slots in the face, (resembling a comb) used for water and sand shots in the late 19th century.

Ribbed: An iron club which was used in the 1920s and 30s, marked with scored ribs and grooves on the face. The feature was eventually banned.

Rubbercore: A rubber-cored ball.

Rubbercored: A ball which has a core of rubber. First manufactured by Coburn Haskell and J.R. Gammeter in 1898, the rubbercore ball featured an interior formed of strip rubber wound around a center and covered with either balata or some similar material. The rubbercored ball replaced the gutta percha.

Rut iron: Alternate names for the iron niblick or track iron, a rut iron was initially used to play out of ruts left by cartwheels.

Sammy: An iron club similar to the jigger, but with a rounded back, used for approach shots.

Sand blaster: A sand wedge.

Sand iron: A heavy, lofted stiff-shafted iron that was designed for play in bunkers.

Sand wedge: An iron club used mostly for "explosion" shots from bunkers. These clubs have a good amount of flange behind and below the leading edge, preventing the clubhead from digging too deeply into the sand. They also have more bounce than other wedges.

Scare: The spliced joint where wooden clubheads were fastened to the shaft before the introduction of drilled sockets near the end of the 19th century.

Arthur F. Knight's infamous Schenectady putter. This putter was banned by the Royal and Ancient Golf Club after Walter Travis used it to win the British Amateur in 1904.

Schenectady or Schenectady putter: This was a center-shafted putter with an aluminum head that was patented by Arthur F. Knight of Schenectady, NY on March 3, 1903. Walter J. Travis used this putter when he won the British amateur championship in 1904, eventually leading to the putter being banned by the Royal and Ancient.

Scoring: The markings of a clubface with grooves, punchmarks, etc.

Scraper: A lofted wood club.

Shaft or clubshaft: The long thin part of a golf club which is attached to the clubhead. Generally made of various woods until the 20th century, when steel replaced wood.

Shallow: A shallow-faced club is relatively narrow from top to bottom, in stark contrast to deep-faced clubs.

Short irons: The higher lofted irons.

Socket: The hosel of an iron clubhead.

Sole: The bottom surface of either an iron or a wooden clubhead.

Soleplate: A metal plate which was screwed to the sole of wooden clubheads.

Spade or spade-mashie: A deep-faced iron club which was more lofted than a mashie.

Spoon: Any group of early wooden clubs which had graduated lofts greater than that of a grassed driver, and accordingly, shorter shafts. The loft on many early clubfaces was usually concaved and resembled the bowled part of a spoon. It is also a term for a wooden club which featured more loft than a brassie in the early 20th century.

Spooned: Lofted.

Spring: Generally referring to the flexibility of a shaft.

Straight-faced: A club with very little loft on the face.

Sweet spot: The perfect spot on a clubface from which to strike the ball.

Swingweight: The measure of the weight of the club in which the shaft and the head are correlated. It is generally desirable to have consistent swingweights in a set of clubs. Clubs generally range from the lightest swingweights A-0 to the heaviest at E-9.

Tee: A tee is a small device, usually made of wood or plastic or rubber, but most commonly wood, on which the ball is placed for driving.

Toe: The end of the clubhead at the point farthest from the shaft.

Torque: The tendency of a clubshaft to twist from the impact of a shot.

Clubmakers and golfers used wax to weatherproof wood shafts.

Track iron: An alternate name for a rut iron or the earliest iron niblick.

Trolley: A British term for a two-wheeled pull cart on which a golf bag is placed and pulled around the course during a round.

Upright: A club having a wide angle of lie where the shaft at address stands relatively close to the vertical position.

Water club: Various patent clubs most popular between the 1880s and the 1930s, which were specifically designed for playing a ball out of the water. These clubs are now banned.

Wedge: A pitching or sand wedge. High lofted clubs used for approach shots to the green.

Whip: The flexibility of a shaft.

Whipping: The binding of thread around the neck of a wooden club. Nylon was later used on the areas where the neck and shaft meet.

Wood: Any club which has a wood head, or material other than wood but the same design characteristics of wooden clubs.

Wry-necked: A British term for a club with a crooked neck or hosel, making the club offset.

Top to bottom: a long-nosed spoon from 1850, a scared bolgin driver from 1885, a bored-through fairway wood from 1903, a bored-through driver from 1903.